THE GREEN BERET GUIDE TO SEVEN GREAT DISASTERS I

WHAT CAUSED THEM AND HOW WE
PREVENT FUTURE ONES

BOB MAYER

Cool Gus Publishing
http://coolgus.com

Cool Gus Publishing
WHO DARES WINS

❀ Created with Vellum

CONTENTS

SHIT DOESN'T JUST HAPPEN

I had to get your attention, just like engineers, soldiers, pilots, astronauts, passengers, policemen, firemen, etc. need to get someone's attention just before a disaster occurs in order to either prevent the event or save lives. Just as engineers, systems analysts, workers, and managers have to get the attention of others in order to point out cascade events that, if unchecked, will lead to a disaster.

Consider the meaning of the phrase. Saying *"shit happens"* indicates events are random, have no meaning and there is no accountability or responsibility. It indicates such events could just as easily happen again and there's nothing we can do about them.

Bull.

This series is about disasters and how to avoid them, mitigate their effects and learn from them. As you will see studying seven significant events in each book, they didn't just happen, and the people and organizations involved weren't helpless victims. Taking the attitude shit happens is potentially fatal. It ignores painful and tragic lessons from the past. If we're going to make the deaths and suffering of victims mean something, we must learn from them.

The bottom line is we can predict and prevent many disasters because every disaster involving human interaction has a man-made factor, a cascade event, involved. In other words, we have control over whether shit happens. But it means changing a complacent mindset, getting rid of delusional thinking, and viewing the world around us in a different way.

2

WHY WRITE THIS BOOK?

I ask "What If" for a living.

What makes Special Forces elite is our planning *before* the actual mission. Planning for all possible contingencies, on top of the actual mission. I did it as an A-Team leader, as a battalion operations officer responsible for deploying 15 A-teams around the world, and as an instructor/writer for many years at the JFK Special Warfare School, which also runs the SERE (Survival, Evasion, Resistance and Escape) school. A large part of that planning is called an Area Study which consists of examining the history not only of the target and enemy, but also similar missions in the past.

I've applied those experiences as a bestselling writer in multiple genres in fiction, including thrillers, historical and science fiction and in nonfiction writing with my *Green Beret Preparation and Survival Guide*, as well as these *Great Disasters* books. In the former I'm looking forward to possible disasters; in the latter I look back at past disasters and dissect them for the cascade events that caused them and examine how similar disasters can be prevented in the future.

In these books I take 'What If' and turn it into 'What Happened' in order to 'What If' similar events in the future.

I've made mistakes.

We all have. And some of us have made mistakes that contributed, either completely or in some percentage, to a *no-do-over*. This is an event where you can't go back and change the result. There has been an irrevocable event. Often these involve death or permanent injury/wounding. You can't undo those.

Soldiers understand this because the environment in which we operate is full of no-do-overs. Special Forces are called Masters of Chaos, but even as Masters, we only control what we control. The best-trained, best equipped, soldier in the world is still only one piece of the entire picture.

That's the part we have to focus on; what we have control over. Our lives play out with many events and tragedies that seem beyond our control, but in which we have some input, some effect. That's what this book highlights, showing you disasters step by step, and how each step teaches us something.

There aren't bad people in these disasters (mostly—bur where there are, their effect is magnified!). They might have made some wrong decisions, but we all have, and the value we can place on them is to learn from them. Sometimes, many of the victims were innocent and not responsible, but we must focus on those who are responsible and in charge and made the key decisions. Or didn't make a key decision.

When I made mistakes, I can look back and have to examine where my part was; where my human error, my lack of focus, my wrong thinking, poor decision-making and ignorance, entered into things. There are things I might not have been able to completely prevent, but if I don't examine my role, I'll never become better at what I do and a better person.

That is why this book exists.

When I was young, I watched the movie *No Highway In The Sky* starring Jimmy Stewart. It's about an engineer who fears the first jet-engine commercial airliner will crash because of metal fatigue. He's so convinced he's right, even though everyone else thinks he's wrong, that he retracts the landing gear while the plane is parked on the runway to prevent it from taking off. Of course, by the end of the movie he's proven right but not in the way he initially thought.

But of more interest, three years after the movie, the first jet passenger plane, the de Havilland Comet had two fatal crashes. The cause: metal fatigue.

Then I went to West Point and after graduation volunteered for the Special Forces (Green Berets). As I'll describe in the Why Listen To Me section, both of these experiences had a profound effect on the way I view the world around me. Operating in the covert world leads one to have a paranoid perspective where shit doesn't just happen, *it's expected*, and we have to prepare for and deal with it.

My wife (who is terrified of flying) and I became very interested in a television show titled *Seconds From Disaster*, which aired on National Geographic. Over the seasons it covered many plane crashes and other disasters. We noticed a startling pattern. No plane crash just happened. There was always a series of mistakes, miscalculations, negligence and other events leading up to those final seconds and the disaster. I call these preceding events: Cascade Events.

> **The Green Beret Guide**
>
> *Cascade Event*
>
> An event prior to the disaster which
> contributes to it,
> but by itself is not disastrous.

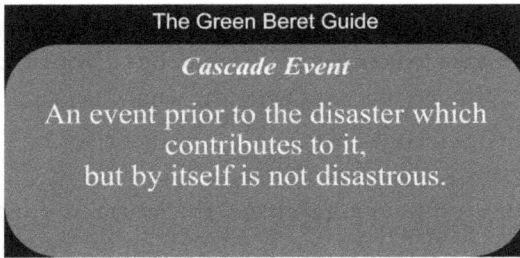

WE STARTED COUNTING these Cascade Events and noticed something else: there were always at least seven. Which led us to develop the:

The Rule of Seven

No human involved disaster happens in isolation or as the result of a single event. It requires a minimum of seven things to go wrong in order for an airplane to crash. And one of those seven is always human error. It might not be the primary cause, but it is always a contributing factor.

This book will show you how the Rule of Seven applies not just to plane crashes, but to disasters across a spectrum of widely different events, from a ship sinking, to a battle that turned into a massacre, to an emigrant party stranded in the wilderness that turned to cannibalism, to the housing bubble that mirrors past bubbles and foreshadows future ones that are inevitable.

The Green Beret Guide

The Rule of Seven

Most disasters require seven things to go
wrong.
If humans are involved, at least one
of those seven cascade events
involves human error.

WHAT CAN we learn from seven disasters that is relevant to
us and could very well save your life and that of others?

We are more powerful than we believe in the face of
disaster.

A disaster involving humans does not happen in
isolation.

In fact, with enough knowledge and preparation, many
individuals and organizations can avoid disasters altogether,
and if caught in one, survive.

Thus, this book is about seven disasters, utilizing the
Rule of Seven to show you seven contributing events to each
disaster and how each one could have been avoided.

That is the purpose of this book.

THREE REASONS TO READ THIS BOOK

Reason one:: False Assumptions

What is a *disaster*?
--The final event of the dramatic action, especially of a tragedy

--An event causing great and often sudden damage or suffering; a disaster

--Utter failure

Note it says the final event of the dramatic action. That means there are things that occurred before, leading to the disaster.

We are usually surprised when a disaster occurs. There is a tendency to believe that a disaster is something that is unexpected, always happens suddenly, and is caused by a single thing going wrong.

These are false assumptions. The vast majority of disasters can easily be predicted with some attention and focus. If predicted, they can often be planned for and averted. If unavoidable, they can be planned for and their results blunted and minimized. Disasters occur suddenly only in terms of the final event, the disaster itself; however, the buildup, via a series of what we will term *cascade events*, can be very long in the unfolding. And at least one of these cascade events involves human error. Thus, most disasters can be avoided.

We will walk through seven well-known disasters, showing the six cascade events leading to the seventh and *final event*. I will list the cascades, pointing out how each could either be noted (knowledge often can prevent the cascade of events that lead to #7, the final event) or corrected. The key for us to focus on is what was learned and changed because of each, saving the lives of countless others afterward.

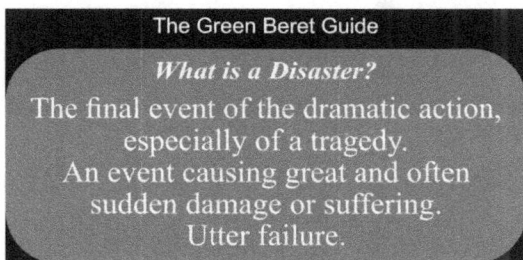

> ### The Green Beret Guide
>
> ### *What is a Disaster?*
> The final event of the dramatic action, especially of a tragedy.
> An event causing great and often sudden damage or suffering.
> Utter failure.

Reason two:: A disaster is closer than you think

While you might not have personally been in a disaster or a tragedy, I can assure you that we have all come close more often than we realize. Many times we've unknowingly been to a #4, #5 or #6 cascade event and not gone into the final event; therein lies one of the key deceptions that lulls us into complacency.

As we will see in the seven examples, there are many places along the cascade of events where a single person saying or doing something, could have stopped the cascade and prevented the disaster or, at the very least, minimized the effect of the final event. Thus, it's very important for us to understand how seemingly innocuous events can play a tragic role if left unchecked. This book is about the *gift of failure*: what we can learn from past disasters in order to avoid ones in the future. The aviation industry works off the gift of failure in that practically every safety innovation introduced is developed in response to a plane crash.

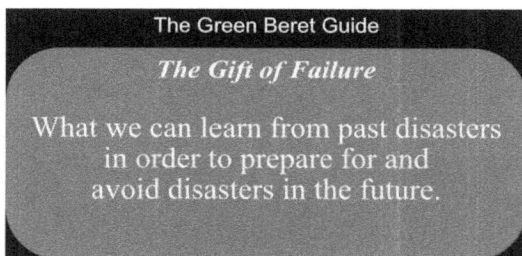

The Green Beret Guide

The Gift of Failure

What we can learn from past disasters in order to prepare for and avoid disasters in the future.

ULTIMATELY, it's about gaining the proper disaster mindset, which goes against our natural instincts because . . .

reason three:: Delusion events fool us

We often look at narrow escapes or near misses as 'fortunate' events where disaster was averted; indeed, we get to the point where we normalize near misses. We need to look at these 'fortunate' events as cascade events where we came close to disaster and were simply lucky that we didn't hit the final event. Relying on luck is a very dangerous mindset yet we immerse ourselves in it on a daily basis. We often call it 'dodging the bullet' forgetting that when a bullet hits, the results are catastrophic to the target. More importantly, the fact a bullet was even fired requires us to pay attention!

We need to focus on cascade events, see their negative potential, and reduce their occurrence. A cascade event that doesn't lead to a final event we will label a *delusion event*. A cascade event and delusion event are exactly the same: the only difference is that a delusion event doesn't result in a final event; a disaster.

This time.

> **The Green Beret Guide**
>
> *Delusion Event*
>
> Also known as "dodging a bullet". A narrow escape or near miss that avoids disaster, which fools us into believing it wasn't an event that *will* eventually lead to disaster.

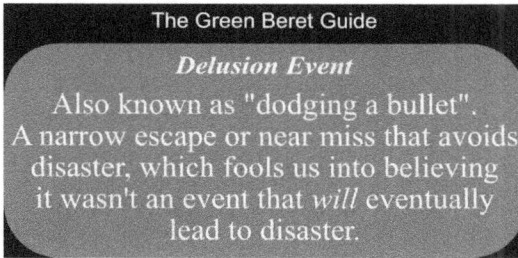

DELUSION EVENTS LEAD us into a delusional mindset: that we will continue to dodge the bullet by doing nothing. In fact, a delusion event, where something goes wrong, but doesn't lead to the final event, reinforces our complacency to do nothing about correcting our error and increases our risk of a final event, a disaster. We take the delusion event as the status quo, not an aberration. Delusion events lead to the normalization of unacceptable risk. For a very simple example, the further you drive with the check engine light on in your car, the more you think it's normal for that the light be on. This is called *normalization* by Diane Vaughan in her book *The Challenger Launch* Decision.(1) We'll discuss this disaster as one of our seven in the second book in this series, focusing on organizational thinking about delusion events.

How many times have you been in a hotel or restaurant or store and the fire alarm goes off? How many times did you rush to the exit? Rather, didn't you, and everyone around you, with no smoke or fire noted, stand around, and wait for someone to actually announce what's going on? We've been desensitized by false alarms to the point where the alarm serves little purpose any longer.

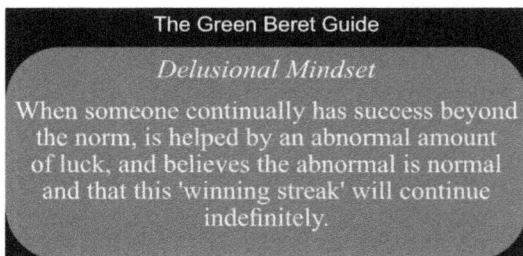

> ### The Green Beret Guide
>
> *Delusional Mindset*
>
> When someone continually has success beyond the norm, is helped by an abnormal amount of luck, and believes the abnormal is normal and that this 'winning streak' will continue indefinitely.

THE HARVARD BUSINESS REVIEW did a study in 2011 (2) and found that delusion events (multiple near misses) preceded *every* disaster and business crisis they studied over a seven-year period. Besides delusional thinking leading to normal-ization, the other problem is *outcome bias*. If you flip a coin six times and it come up heads six times, even though statis-tically rare (1 chance in 64 attempts), you will tend to start focusing on the result, believing all coin tosses end up heads. While we know this isn't true, we tend to base our probabilities of future occurrences not on the statistics of reality but on our experiences.

This is called heuristics and is at the root of many disasters. *Heuristics* is experience-based techniques for learning and problem solving that give a solution which isn't necessarily optimal. We generalize based on the things we value most: our own experience and information related to us from sources we trust. Think how many 'truths' you have heard that turn out to be nothing more than an urban legend or a superstition. Yet we base many of our daily and emergency actions around these.

A small example from *The Green Beret Preparation and Survival Guide*: every so often there is a news article about someone in a desperate survival situation who claims drinking their urine helped them survive. The truth is that's absolutely the wrong thing to do. But it's one of those stories that gets repeated enough, until we believe it to be true. Because we only hear from survivors, who lived in spite of doing the wrong thing. Dead people don't get to tell their story. Except when we study how they died which is one of the goals of this book; we must cherish their gift.

RANGER

DO NOT DRINK THE FOLLOWING:

Seawater: it is 4 percent salt. It takes 2 quarts of bodily fluids to rid the body of 1 quart of seawater. Thus you are actually dehydrating yourself twice as fast.
Sea Ice: same as seawater.
Blood: Is considered a food, since it's salty, and requires additional bodily fluids to process. It might also transmit disease.
Urine: 2% salt and contains harmful body wastes. There's a reason your body is getting rid of it.
Alcoholic beverages: They dehydrate you and cloud your judgment.

From *The Green Beret Preparation and Survival Guide*

IT IS human nature that we focus on successful outcomes much more than negative ones. It's irrational, but that's part of being human. In the same way, managers and leaders are taught to plan for success, not failure, since it's believed planning for failure is negative thinking. In fact, I would submit that many people are part of a cult of positive thinking that often excludes reality.

The good news is we tend to be predictably irrational and understanding and accepting our tendency to make a cascade event a delusion event, is the first step in correcting this problem.

References

Diane Vaughan *The Challenger Launch Decision: Risky Technology, Culture and Deviancy at NASA*, University of Chicago Press (April 15, 1997)

HARVARD BUSINESS REVIEW: How To Avoid Disaster; Catherine H. Tinsley, Robin L. Dillon, and Peter M. Madsen. April 2011.

4

WHY TO LISTEN TO ME?

I trained for, lived in, and succeeded in a chaotic environment in two careers: As a Special Operations soldier and making a living as a novelist.

I don't have a PhD in engineering or an MBA (I do have an MFA). I did earn a perfect score on the Systems Engineering final at West Point, but I majored in psychology. I have a unique background, having graduated the Military Academy, served in the Infantry and Special Forces including commanding an A-Team, being a battalion operations officer, and teaching at the JFK Special Warfare Center and School. I am a best-selling author in the creative field of fiction across multiple genres including thriller, science fiction, historical and romance, and in the practical field of non-fiction. I'm also a consultant applying Special Forces strategies and tactics to a variety of businesses and organizations as well as doing survival consulting and Area Studies.

Here are the three reasons my expertise contributes to this subject:

Reason One:: West Point trains for, and Special Operations functions in, Chaos and Disaster

Disaster planning in the civilian world is primarily the province of engineers and management. The problem with that is engineers and management are trained for, plan for, and work in a controlled environment (what they *think* is a controlled environment). Thus, delusion events are outside their comfort zone; aberrations. In fact, as we will see, engineers and managers are often trained to be blind to cascade events. Their training and work environment normally do not reward focusing on cascade events, but rather punishes it.

West Point is an extraordinarily controlled environment. Things run almost perfectly there; so much so that graduates often have problems adjusting to the 'real' Army they go into. But West Point also has over 200 years of experience training leaders and preparing soldiers for war. War, by its very definition is chaos and disaster. This accumulation of institutional knowledge is inculcated in cadets in a high-pressure cauldron of mental, physical and emotional stress for four years.

(Of course, sometimes it doesn't take, as we will see with one of the events we cover in this book that focuses on one of our more notorious graduates.)

Special Operations soldiers train for war. War is called controlled chaos; an incessant series of cascade events. War might be considered the ultimate disaster and combat a final event. In order to prepare for this final event, Special Operations soldiers train for, plan for, and work in a stressful environment every day.

Mentally, the most difficult training I went through was Robin Sage, the final exercise in the Special Forces Qualification Course. Robin Sage is where a team of students is sent into isolation to plan, and then infiltrates into the North Carolina countryside to conduct a guerrilla warfare exercise. A critical component of Robin Sage is to put prospective Green Berets in lose-lose scenarios. This is a training scenario where there is no 'right' solution. Rigid minds are often unable to think creatively while under stress and lose-lose training quickly determines someone's capabilities.

Thinking outside of the immediate situation is important in preparing for and averting disasters. Do you remember in the Star Trek movie (*Wrath of Khan*) and the *Kobayashi Maru* simulator program? The basic problem and the opening of the movie was set up this way: A Star Fleet ship, which the student commands, is patrolling near the neutral zone. A distress call is received from a disabled Federation vessel inside the neutral zone. An enemy warship is approaching from the other side. A vessel more powerful than the one the student commands. The choices seem obvious: ignore the distress call (which violates the law of space) or go to its aid (violating the neutral zone) and face almost certain destruction from the enemy vessel. Obviously, both choices are bad.

What Kirk did was sneak into the computer center the night before he was scheduled to go through the simulation and change the parameters so that he could successfully save the vessel without getting destroyed. Would you have thought of that? Was it cheating? If you ain't cheating you ain't trying. It's not cheating when it succeeds.

A key to lose-lose training is you get to see how someone reacts when they are wrong or fail. Lose-lose training is a good way to put people in a crisis. Frustration can often lead to anger, which can lead to failure or enlightenment.

> **The Green Beret Guide**
>
> *Lose-Lose Training*
> Aka: *Kobayashi Maru* scenario.
> A training scenario where there is no
> 'right' or 'good' solution.
> The goal is to understand how someone
> thinks and decides.

IF A DISASTER STRUCK, whom would you want at your side helping you? A doctor? Lawyer? Policeman? Engineer? MBA? Teacher? While they all have special skills, I submit that the overwhelming choice might well be a Special Forces Green Beret. Someone trained in survival, medicine, weapons, tactics, communications, engineering, counter-terrorism, tactical and strategic intelligence, and with the capability to be a force multiplier.

Most important, you want someone who has been hand-picked, survived rigorous training, and has the positive mental outlook to not only survive, but thrive in chaos, and knows how to be part of a team. Green Berets have been called Masters of Chaos. Every Green Beret is also a leader.

A key to dealing with disasters is leadership, not management. Often, in order to deal with a cascade event, leadership and courage are needed to go against a management culture of complacency and fear. As we will see in each disaster, fear is a factor in at least one, if not more, cascade events. This fear runs the gamut from job security fear, to social fear, to physical fear. Few people want to be the 'boy/girl who cries wolf' even when they see a pack of wolves. What's even harder is when we're the only one who sees the wolf in sheep's clothing.

I've written this book to help individuals and organizations avoid disasters, but I come at it from a different direction as a former Special Operations soldier. In the Special Forces (Green Berets) the key to our successful missions was the planning. The preparation.

In isolation we war-gamed as many possible disaster situations we could imagine for our upcoming mission and prepared as well as we could for them. In fact, we *expected* things to go wrong, a very different mindset from that of engineers and management. We were firm believers in Murphy's Law: What can go wrong, will. In other words: Shit will happen.

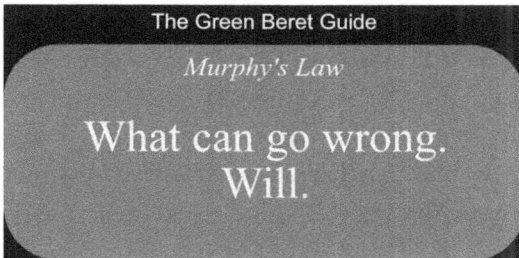

The Green Beret Guide
Murphy's Law
What can go wrong.
Will.

OUR JOB WAS to plan for possibilities, avoid cascade events, and if they did occur have a plan to deal with it.

Reason two:: Less is better

This book is short and to the point. There are thousands of disasters I could have drawn from. I focus on these seven in this first book in order to give focus. Each is representative of a type of disaster. We can extrapolate the disaster to similar circumstances, but the key is to understand the overall concept of having a disaster mindset. Further books in this series will cover other disasters, with the lessons learned from each. As we go through more and more disaster we will see patterns. Since there are an infinite number of possible scenarios and cascade events, the goal is to learn to adopt a mindset rather than focus on specific solutions.

I don't go into much detail on each of the cascade events of each disaster. I list them, with a timeline, a brief explanation, and then a comment on the lesson learned from each cascade event leading up to the final event. The goal is to have a cumulative impact on your mindset as you go through disaster after disaster. This book is about a mindset because there is no way to cover every possible scenario. Each of you is in a unique situation and face unique challenges. You must learn the disaster mindset and then apply it to your environment and circumstances and also be prepared for the unexpected because disasters often strike in unexpected ways.

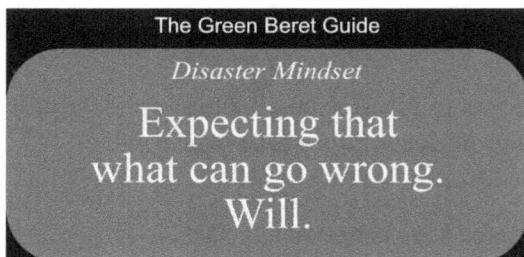

The Green Beret Guide

Disaster Mindset

Expecting that what can go wrong. Will.

THIS IS why I also cover the Area Study in this book at the end, after you've learned about these seven disasters. It's something that I go into more detail in **The Green Beret Preparation and Survival Guide**, but it's the first step of focusing preparation. Study your specific situation for potential disasters.

There are also 'asides' throughout this book marked by the Special Forces patch and italicized font. They are interesting tidbits from personal experience or other events that I've put in as an added benefit.

I chose some significant disasters that almost everyone has heard of. (Unfortunately, the two teenage girls behind me when I went to see the movie *Titanic* were not aware the ship was going to sink. They were quite distraught when it did.) These are events that echo in our collective consciousness.

Reason three:: The HALO effect

HALO stands for High Altitude Low Opening parachuting. We jump above 25,000 feet and fall. A long way. Then open the parachute at a low altitude. In other words, it stands for starting far away and zooming in on something from the outside.

This is the term I use when I consult for a business foreign to me, like IT. When I walk in to an IT company I know pretty much nothing about how they do things (I know how to turn on my computer, but that's about it). But that gives me an advantage because I have no pre-conceived notions about how things should be done. I am not going to reinvent the wheel, the way most organizations periodically do. I am thinking outside the box because I was never in the box to begin with. This is what I mean when I say HALO;

step back from your environment and look at it with a completely different perspective: one of potential disaster.

For potential disasters, as we will see, an outside perspective often lacks the dangerous, closed mindsets that often permeate organizations. An outsider is also free of internal pressures, politics, and critiques. An outsider can see delusion events as possible cascade events. An outsider is free of the chain of command/management and is able to express concerns. An outsider is trained differently than insiders and has a different perspective.

The Green Beret Guide

The HALO Effect

Looking at something from 'outside the box' which gives a fresh and unique perspective that isn't prejudiced by prior experience and knowledge.

THREE BENEFITS OF DISASTER
THINKING, PLANNING & PREPARING

As a Green Beret, I was focused on two main reasons for disaster planning and preparation. As a writer, I learned about a third, more subtle benefit of disaster planning in order to have a successful career in a field where 99% of those entering eventually fail.

You Disaster Plan for three reasons

1. To avoid the disaster. Since at least one of the six cascade events leading to the disaster is human error, if we plan and prepare adequately, we can delete the human error cascade event from the situation, thus avoiding the final event.

2. To have a plan, equipment, training etc. in place in case the disaster strikes. If we project out possible disasters, we can prepare for their eventuality. I am adamant that preparation is critical, even more so than actual actions during the disaster. It is too late when we reach a disaster to prepare for it. Even the best-trained individual will be overwhelmed

by a disaster if they have not prepared for it. In the last disaster we cover in this book, we'll see how the fact someone planned for possible disasters helped avert a terrible one.

3. To give you peace of mind in day-to-day living so you don't constantly have to worry about potential disasters because you are prepared for them. This allows you to experience a higher quality of life. You've done your best to avoid the disaster, making the likelihood that much less. Since you've done your best to prepare for the disaster, you can focus on other things; like succeeding. Too many people worry about potential disasters without preparing; this is a fundamental failure and fuels fear. Fear feeds on itself and is debilitating. Often, extreme fear can bring about an event that would have never occurred otherwise. Confident people are prepared people.

DISASTER 1: TITANIC
SYSTEMATIC FAILURE

"There is no danger that Titanic will sink. The boat is unsinkable and nothing but inconvenience will be suffered by the passengers."
Phillip Franklin, White Star Line vice-president, 1912

Titanic is a classic example of systematic cascade events, many apparently unrelated to each other, any of which if corrected, would have averted the final event.

The Facts

The Titanic sank in the early morning of 15 April 1912 after hitting an iceberg in the North Atlantic. The official death toll is 1,517 making it #5 on the all-time fatality list for shipwrecks. What makes this sinking notable is that the Titanic was the largest ship afloat at the time of its maiden voyage and was declared 'unsinkable' by its builders.

The Timeline

Roughly 1,000 BC: Snow falls on Greenland, which will eventually become the iceberg the *Titanic* strikes.

31 July 1908: Plans for Number 400 (*Olympic*) are presented to the White Star Line and approved. Number 401 (*Titanic*) is also approved.

31 March 1909: Construction begins on *Titanic*.

1909: The fatal iceberg calves off a glacier on the west coast of Greenland.

31 May 1911: Number 401 slides on 22 tons of soap and tallow into the water. It is not christened or formally named, keeping with White Star tradition.

2 April 1912: First sea trials of *Titanic*.

10 April 1912: *Titanic* sets out on her first, and last, voyage.

14 April 1912; 11:40 pm: *Titanic* strikes an iceberg.

15 April 1912; 2:20 am: *Titanic* sinks.

The Cascading Events

Cascade One

An unusual weather pattern caused more icebergs than usual and forced the ship farther south than normal.

The actual piece of ice that struck the *Titanic* was formed about three thousand years ago, beginning with snowfall on the western coast of Greenland. Compressed into ice, then slowly pushed downward and outward as part of a glacier, the iceberg calved into the open ocean roughly about the time the keel of the *Titanic* was laid in Ireland, thus setting two objects, thousands of miles apart, on an inexorable collision course.

Inexorable only if the next six events occur.

The iceberg made a rather difficult and highly unlikely journey, from Greenland, to Baffin Bay, to the Davis Strait, to the Labrador Sea and finally into the North Atlantic. Less than one percent of icebergs calved in a year make it that far. By the time it struck the *Titanic* it was over 5,000 miles from its origin. It also had less than two years of existence left.

Extraordinary bad luck that it made it that far.

But it did.

Lesson

Expect the expected. The icebergs were farther south, but it was also April, the worst iceberg month. It was well known as the season went on that it was a bad year for icebergs in the North Atlantic. Thus, while it was unusual, it wasn't really unexpected that the *Titanic* encountered one during this trip.

Cascade Two

Rivets were of inferior material, some put in by inexperienced welders, causing more damage during the collision than should have occurred.

While many believe the hole ripped into the *Titanic* by the iceberg was huge, there were actually six small gashes, totaling 3.2 square feet or less than one square meter. That is an incredibly small group of holes for such a large ship, totaling an area less than the size of your kitchen table. But the holes were stretched out along the side of the ship pouring water into six of sixteen watertight compartments: if four flooded, the ship was doomed. Additionally, the 'watertight' compartments were only that in terms of bottom and horizontal. They were open on the top.

If only the metal hide of the mighty ship had been able to block just three of those small punctures? But there were two major reasons why it couldn't.

The iron rivets were class 3 (best) instead of 4 (best-best). If one is building the greatest ship of the time, one should be using the highest quality material.

As shear forces were brought to bear when the hull plates hit the iceberg, the rivets broke. In fact, the Cunard Line, which built the *Lusitania*, had been using steel rivets for several years. The company in charge of building the *Titanic*, used some steel rivets on the *Titanic*, but only in the core of the ship, not the bow and side where the collision would take place.

Why were inferior rivets, the glue that holds a ship together, used? Because of insufficient supply. While constructing *Titanic*, the builder was simultaneously building its sister ships, *Olympia* and *Britannica* which limited supply. Ambitious plans automatically bring greater risk.

Building the three largest ships ever, all at the same time, in the same shipyard, stretched not only supply of material beyond safety limits, but the availability of skilled workers. At every meeting held by the company up to the completion of the ship, the lack of skilled welders was brought up as a problem. Welding by hand is an art form, and there is no doubt that some of those extra workers hired to do this critical job lacked the necessary experience. Given the way ships were constructed at the time, welders were absolutely essential for proper and safe construction.

For decades after the sinking, the builder fought the accusation that the bolts were substandard. But now, examination of rivets brought up from the wreckage proves that they contained four times as much slag than they should have, making them fragile. In essence, the ship was doomed before it even touched water. On top of that, the cold water made the inferior metal even more brittle.

Lesson

Set realistic goals and don't skimp on the cost of construction. Class 4 rivets should have been used at the very least, if not steel. Even more key was over-reaching in construction. Building the world's three largest ships at the same time inevitably caused shortages of material and skilled labor. Yet, this did not deter the company from doing it. They set a goal, which exceeded safe capacity and many paid the price for it.

Cascade Three

Lack of a sufficient number of lifeboats for the crew and passengers.

Titanic carried enough lifeboats to accommodate 1,178 people; for a ship with a capacity three times that. It must be understood that at the time, the theory was that lifeboats were considered that per se. They were transfer boats, as it was believed that if needed, there would be time to radio for help, and then transfer all passengers and crew to the responding vessels. In fact, the lifeboat capacity for *Titanic* exceeded that which was legally required at the time: British vessels over 10,000 tons had to carry at least 16 lifeboats with capacity for 50% of passengers and crew. The *Titanic* exceeded this requirement by having a capacity for 52% of the people on board.

Unfortunately, there wasn't a focus on the 48% that weren't provided for.

Plus, the *Titanic* displaced 52,000 tons, more than five times that maximum. By constructing the largest vessel at the time, the builder was outstripping maritime law. As we push the limits of technology and construction, constantly going for bigger and faster, there is a need to be self-regulating in terms of safety.

The *Titanic* carried 20 lifeboats. 14 were wooden with a capacity of 65 each. 4 were collapsible boats (wooden bottom, canvas sides) with a capacity of 47 each. There were also two cutters with a capacity of 40 each.

Interestingly, the *Titanic* had 16 sets of davits, each of which was capable of handling 4 lifeboats. Doing the math, this gives the ship the capacity to carry 62 boats (62 boats x 65 capacity equals 4,030 people). The original design for the *Titanic* called for 48 lifeboats, which would have held 3,120 people. But that number was reduced to 16 for various reasons (including esthetics as some of those additional lifeboats would have blocked the view from the deck).

Lesson

When technology outstrips current safety requirements, one should not take the easy way and adhere to outdated laws. The reality of the new technology requires a new reality in safety requirements.

After the *Titanic* sinking, naturally, the lifeboat requirement was changed so that a ship was required to carry enough lifeboats for its capacity, a common sense requirement that should have been organically implemented by designers and builders as ships grew larger.

Sadly, while the *Titanic*'s lifeboats had the capacity for 1,178 people, there were only 706 survivors.

To rely on simply obeying the law when dealing with

safety issues, one leaves things open to a final event that will require the law to be changed after the fact.

It should not require death to update safety requirements.

Here is a snippet from the United States Senate inquiry:

"There was no system adopted for loading the boats; there was great indecision as to the deck from which boats were to be loaded; there was wide diversity of opinion as to the number of the crew necessary to man each boat; there was no direction whatever as to the number of passengers to be carried by each boat, and no uniformity in loading them. On one side only women and children were put in the boats, while on the other side there was almost an equal proportion of men and women put into the boats, the women and children being given the preference in all cases. The failure to utilize all lifeboats to their recognized capacity for safety unquestionably resulted in the needless sacrifice of several hundred lives which might otherwise have been saved."

Cascade Four

The two lookouts in the crows nest didn't have binoculars.

The very definition of lookout means that one must look out. Yet, the two men in the highest part of the ship, with the greatest vantage point, didn't have access to binoculars just feet away from them because the key to the locker holding the devices had left the ship before sailing.

The key was held by David Blair, an officer who was reassigned just before the *Titanic* sailed. He failed to turn over the key to the box holding this equipment.

One of the lookouts, Fred Fleet, survived and told the official enquiry he had no doubt that he would have spotted the iceberg earlier if he'd had binoculars. When asked how much earlier, he said that it would have been in "enough time to get out of the way."

Aside: Curiously, ninety-five years after the sinking, the key and a postcard from Blair indicating his disappointment at missing the sailing sold at auction for almost $200,000.

Lesson

Key equipment is just that: key.

Pun inevitable.

To realize an essential piece of gear isn't available should raise a red flag, not a shrug. Just because the key wasn't available, doesn't mean they couldn't have broken open the box and gotten to the binoculars. But institutional inertia was at work here: the lookouts didn't want to complain up the chain of command and be labeled trouble-makers. No news is good news.

Not.

Even if they didn't break in and get the essential equipment, there is no doubt someone else on board this ship had a set. After all, a number of lifeboats were left off from the original design in order to improve the view from the deck. Surely a number of passengers, and probably even some officers or the crew, had telescopes or binoculars. But once more, inertia kept these from being sought out.

An organization has to establish an environment of openness where potential problems can be raised before they become cascade events, particularly with regard to safety equipment.

Curiously, in researching this cascade event, many articles and reports end by saying that the binoculars would have been of limited use on the night in question; but all reports from the time state that the night in question was perfectly clear with almost unlimited visibility. And one of the two lookouts says they would have helped.

I'll go with the guy who was there.

Cascade Five

Speed kills. We hear that all the time, but there are so many variations of this, it's amazing how often it is forgotten. The ship was going too fast for the conditions. The deadliest airplane disaster in history (two 747s colliding on a runway) had as a cascade event one of the pilots being in a rush.

While some have claimed that Captain Smith was trying to set a cross-Atlantic record, the reality is the *Titanic* didn't have the capability to break the established record. Plus, it was traveling the southern route, which is longer than the northern route on which the record had been established.

I believe it was more of a mindset harkening to the size of the *Titanic* and the belief in her invulnerability. Also, as it was the maiden voyage, there had to be a desire to show what the ship was capable of. Have you ever noticed how much of a rush people are in when they're traveling? Whether it be by ship, plane, train, or automobile, people push the limits of speed as if arriving a few seconds, minutes, hours were all that critical when balanced against safety. They're willing to trade their life in order to make that next stoplight by accelerating through the yellow.

On top of that desire for speed by Captain Smith, was a delusional mindset. Each day the ship encountered no problem, the faster it went. On the first day, *Titanic* covered 386 miles. Day two: 519. Day 3: 546.

While the overall record was out of the question, there is the possibility that Captain Smith was trying to better the crossing time of his sister ship, *Olympia*, on the same route. Also consider this: Captain Smith, at the beginning of this maiden voyage, might well have been at the start of the last voyage in his career as he had only one more crossing to make in order to reach retirement. Personnel near the end of their careers can act in unpredictable ways. They might want to make a statement, in either a positive or a negative way.

The bottom line was that the *Titanic* was warned several times of icebergs in the area (more on this under wireless). The ship was sailing full speed into an area with obstacles. With lookouts who didn't have binoculars.

A ship that massive is very slow to turn and even slower to stop. During sea trials, the *Titanic* required 850 yards to come to a halt from full speed. And 3,850 yards to turn around. Captain Smith was driving his ship faster than the ship could respond to an obstacle; a formula for disaster. Do you see how the speed cascade event piles on top of the binocular event? And on top of the upcoming wireless event?

Interestingly, the captain of the *Californian*, who was castigated for not coming to the aid of the sinking *Titanic*, was in the position to possibly do so because he had stopped his ship for the night, feeling the iceberg field was too thick to attempt in the dark. He had also sent out a warning about the ice field that *Titanic* received.

Another mindset that might come into play here is the concept of putting danger behind as quickly as possible. While illogical, speeding through an ice field meant less time spent *in* the ice field, which one might believe reduces that possibility of a collision. In reality, speed is only a negative factor in this scenario.

It should be noted that Captain Smith wasn't alone in going full speed into an ice field. At the time, many large ships operated at speed, relying on ice warnings from other ships and lookouts. Since both of those are other cascade events, you can see how this cascade event was predicated on false assumptions.

There is no doubt that Captain Smith, and many other ship captains of the era, believed ice was not that great a danger to such a well-constructed ship. In 1907, a German liner had hit an iceberg head-on but still been able to finish its crossing. In that same year, Smith declared that he could not "imagine any condition which would cause a ship to founder. Modern shipbuilding has gone beyond that."

Lesson

Human error via speed.

'Slow down' is a mantra that works more often than 'speed up' does. Many human-initiated disasters are the direct result of speed. And not just in a conveyance moving too fast. Speed is dangerous in inspections, decision-making, production, and many other areas.

Paradoxically, Captain Smith was slow in his decision to order the ship to be abandoned. It took 45 minutes from the time Smith was told the ship was going to sink for the first lifeboat to be launched; and it was only partly full. It took another hour and twenty minutes for the last lifeboat to be launched. When speed was critical, Smith and his crew didn't deliver.

Cascade Six

Warnings were ignored and the wireless radio wasn't used correctly

The wireless radio on the *Titanic* was the most powerful in the world at the time. Its normal working range was guaranteed for 250 miles, but during daylight, it could often reach 400 miles. Interestingly, the range was much greater at night, reaching out to 2,000 miles. This is bolstered by the fact that the two radio operators had watches that went from 8 pm to 2 am and 2 am to 8 am. They were not on duty during the day.

Thus, the wireless was engaged in transmitting messages to New York City during the *Night To Remember*, as the communiques had piled up all day long. In fact, passenger communication was such a priority that when the *Californian* tried to radio about encountering ice, the *Titanic*'s operator replied with "Shut Up!"

This was because all the ships used the same frequency and the incoming message was jamming the *Titanic*'s outgoing messages. This single frequency also caused problems after the iceberg was struck as *Titanic*'s messages about its condition and location were often garbled by inquiries from other ships about what was going on. There was no set procedure to handle the newly implemented SOS.

Another problem with the *Californian*'s message was that it didn't include the ship's position. Warning that they were surrounded by ice, but not giving location, pretty much negated the effectiveness of the message (how often do we forget to tell people where we are?). Also, the message was not sent with the proper MSG code that would have insured it was given to Captain Smith.

After being told to shut up, the radio operator on the *Californian* simply turned off his set and went to sleep, thus never receiving the *Titanic's* calls for help.

Titanic received numerous warnings from other ships in the area of drifting ice. Despite that, the cascading event of full speed ahead continued. The wireless wasn't officially under the command of the ship. It was run by the Marconi company and designed more for passenger messages than ship's operations. In essence, passenger messages were a priority over ship's message.

Lesson

Lack of standing operating procedures with regard to the radio caused its ability to warn to be ineffective, and its ability to secure rescue after the final event to be minimal.

While the most powerful radio was built into the *Titanic*, it was viewed more as a passenger amenity rather than an integral part of the ship and key to its safe operation. When we prioritize amenity over safety, the results can be catastrophic.

Another example of this kind of cascade event is Swissair III where sparks arcing in a newly installed in-flight entertainment system led to a fire that eventually led to the plane to crash.

Cascade Seven: Final Event: DISASTER

At 11:40 PM on the 14th of April 1912, the *Titanic* struck an iceberg, causing fatal damage to the ship. It sank at 2:20 am on the 15th of April.

Once the ship hit that iceberg, many of the cascade events had an effect. Lack of lifeboats and poor wireless operation being two key ones. The evacuation of the ship was poorly executed and supervised. Some lifeboats left not fully loaded. There were 705 survivors of *Titanic* and 1,517 casualties. But doing the math, with lifeboats the ship did have, with a potential capacity of 1,178 we are left with at least 473 unfilled spaces on those lifeboats. On such a calm night, the boats could have been overloaded with more.

In essence, studying the 2 hours and 40 minutes between the strike and boat slipping beneath the waves, one finds little evidence of a coordinated attempt to save passengers. No makeshift rafts were built. No coordination was made with the lifeboats being launched. Wireless signals were intermittent and often over-ridden by other ships.

Inquiries were, of course, launched. In Great Britain, it was the longest and most detailed inquiry in history up to that time. The United States also launched an inquiry. Both came to roughly the same conclusions:

More lifeboats were needed. Maritime law was changed as a result.

The lifeboats were not adequately filled or crewed.

Captain Smith did not heed the ice warnings received.

The bottom line was that the collision was the result of steaming too fast in an ice field.

Later in this book, we'll discuss how important a survival instinct and thought process is to disasters, but a little-known fact is that a cook from the *Titanic* survived in the water for over 2 hours before he was rescued. Almost everyone else in the water died. The difference? The cook kept swimming to keep his body temperature up.

As a graduate of the Danish Royal Navy Fromandkorpset Combat Swim School, and subsequently commanding a maritime operations specialty Green Beret A-Team, I have, unfortunately,

experience in cold water. While many people succumb quickly in cold water, having the determination to overcome the stunning, initial shock of entering near-ice water, and following it up with constant movement, one increases the length of time they can survive.

THE UNITED STATES inquiry concluded that all those involved had followed the standards of shipping as set at the time. The disaster was therefore an "act of God." In essence, the British inquiry reached the same point, noting that Captain Smith had not done anything particularly unusual, following long-standing practices of the time, which had not previously been shown to be unsafe. After all, British ships had carried over 3.5 million passengers in the decade before the *Titanic* with only 10 fatalities.

Ultimately, they were following delusion events, making a disaster like the *Titanic* inevitable.

As we move on to the next disaster it is interesting to reflect on a quote from the British inquiry: "*What was a mistake in the case of the Titanic would without doubt, be negligence in any similar case in the future.*"

Summary

Hubris is the making of tragedy and the *Titanic* was one of the greatest tragedies.

Other than Cascade One, the forming of and calving of the iceberg, ever cascade was a result of systemic human error that led to the sinking of the Titanic.

7

DISASTER 2: LITTLE BIG HORN

LEADERSHIP FAILURE

"There are not enough Indians in the world to defeat the Seventh Cavalry."
George Armstrong Custer

Overall, we don't like failure. There are many books are out there with 'success' in the title, but we are loath to study the flip side.

However, Americans do celebrate failures of a certain type, especially in combat. Whether it is the Alamo, Little Big Horn, or others, we love the drama of the Last Stand.

What we need to do is learn from the failures that led to these desperate situations and avoid them in the future. Usually there is a failure of leadership involved. George Armstrong Custer's career culminated on that fateful day on the Greasy Grass River in Montana, but the seeds of that massacre were sown long before, and far away from that place and time.

To analyze the cascade events that culminated in

Custer's Massacre (or Lakota Victory Day, depending on your perspective) we have to look at events strategic (big picture) and tactical (small picture).

The Facts

On 25 June 1876, 5 of the 12 companies of the US 7th Cavalry under George Armstrong Custer's command were annihilated by a combined force of Lakota Sioux, Northern Cheyenne and Arapahoe Native Americans under the leadership of Crazy Horse and Gall.

The Timeline

1861: Custer graduates West Point.

27 November 1868: The Battle of Washita River.

2 August 1874: Custer reports finding gold 'right from the grass roots' in the Black Hills.

25 JUNE 1876;

10:50 am: Custer decides to attack the Native American encampment on the Little Big Horn River.

12:12 pm: First divide of Custer's command as Benteen's column splits off.

2:15 pm: Second divide of Custer's command as Reno's column splits off. Reno quickly becomes engaged in battle.

3:33 pm: Reno's command retreats into the trees along the Little Big Horn River, hard pressed by the Native Americans.

3:56 pm: Custer's companies advance down Medicine Tail Coulee.

5:00 pm: Last of heavy firing heard from Custer's position.

The Cascading Events

Cascade One

West Point, Civil War, and Indian War records of George Armstrong Custer foretold a leader big on ego, bravery, and foolishness.

The best predictor of future behavior is past behavior. Custer graduated last in his class of 34 at West Point. He is quoted as saying that since there were only two places in a class, the head, or the foot, and he had no inspiration to be the head, he might as well be the foot. We called that person the 'goat' at West Point. Graduating as the goat means walking a very, very fine line between being kicked out and hanging on. As Custer's 'Last Stand' is celebrated, the goat of each class is celebrated at the Academy. In my year, each member of the class donated $1 to be given to the goat when he/she received their diploma. It wasn't just academics which were Custer's bane. He also received numerous demerits and punishment tours, many for pulling pranks on other cadets.

Right after graduating, Custer failed as duty officer when he didn't stop a fight between two cadets. He was court-martialed (not for the last time) and it was only because of the outbreak of the Civil War that he wasn't dismissed from the Army. We must remember that extreme circumstances sometimes allow personnel who would otherwise be weeded out to be passed through the system designed to stop them.

These West Point legacies indicate three things:

While it might denote laziness, it actually indicates a desire for the excitement of living on the edge.

Custer felt he could determine what was important (having fun and doing what he wanted) and what wasn't (academics and discipline).

Custer viewed West Point as a stepping-stone to something next and bigger without inculcating the standards and teachings and discipline.

SUCH A POOR RECORD would have exiled Custer to the worst posting in his class, probably an isolated frontier or west coast fort, where he would have languished in quiet ignominy. But timing is everything. Custer's class, originally the class of 1862, was graduated a year early due to the outbreak of the Civil War. Perhaps if he'd spent the full four years at the Academy, Custer might not have even graduated.

Custer became one of the youngest generals ever in the history of the US Army, reaching that rank at only 23. He went straight from captain to general, despite having no command experience. He took charge of a brigade, a unit several times larger than that he would command later at the Little Big Horn (in fact, the 7th Cavalry was the smallest unit Custer ever commanded).

While he was promoted rapidly, earning the admiration of higher-ranking officers for his dash and willingness to take chances, his men had a different view on things. Percentage-wise his cavalry unit had one of the highest number of casualties of any over the course of the Civil War.

It must be noted that Custer didn't just risk their lives, he also risked his own. He was always out front, leading the way, with a disregard for personal danger, or danger to his men. At Gettysburg, Custer led the battle against JEB Stuart's cavalry when the Confederates tried to flank Union positions. He commanded a charge where he lost more than any other Union cavalry brigade, but won the battle. Afterward, he didn't reflect on the cost, but rather wrote in his report: "*I challenge the annals of warfare to produce a more brilliant or successful charge of cavalry.*"

He was crucial in the war's last campaign, helping surround General Robert E. Lee's forces at Appomattox. General Sheridan was so grateful that he gifted Custer the desk on which the surrender was signed.

Even Custer acknowledged that he needed a lot of luck to have survived the Civil War and all the headlong charges he led, but that didn't stop him from continuing to do it. Luck repeated becomes habit, and leads beyond delusional thinking to a *delusional mindset*. This is where someone who has had success far beyond that which should be the norm, helped with an abnormal amount of luck, believes the abnormal is normal and that their streak will continue indefinitely.

> ### The Green Beret Guide
> *Delusional Mindset*
>
> When someone continually has success beyond the norm, is helped by an abnormal amount of luck, and believes the abnormal is normal and that this 'winning streak' will continue indefinitely.

PEACETIME, as it is to many generals who blossomed in combat (think Patton) was not welcomed by, or kind to, Custer. He was reduced in rank and went from commanding a brigade to technically being the second in command of the 7th Cavalry Regiment. Since the actual commander of the regiment didn't take to the field, Custer became the defacto commander.

My first duty assignment in the Army was with the 12th Cavalry of the 1st Cavalry Division. We rode armored vehicles, not horses. And the unit down the road from us was the 7th Cavalry, still with the Gary Owen crest.

IN 1867, Custer led the 7th Cavalry against the Plains Indians with little success. Bored, and perhaps lonely, without authorization, Custer left his command in the field and rode back to Fort Riley, Kansas to visit his wife. He was promptly placed under arrest for being AWOL. He was court-martialed and found guilty. His sentence was a one-year suspension from the Army without pay. For a leader who demanded absolute obedience from his subordinates (to the point of ordering summary executions of soldiers for desertion, the same crime he committed), this is a rather amazing incident and very telling about Custer's character. Custer played by his own rules; not the Army's or anyone else's.

The problem with playing by your own rules is that reality ultimately catches up to you. No person is larger than the world around them. *House Rules* for disasters is reality.

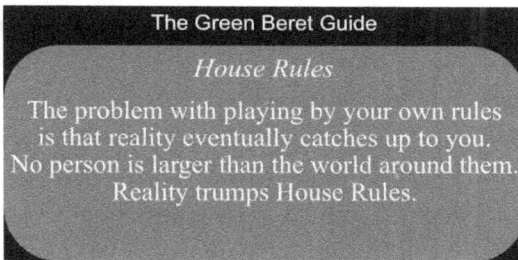

The Green Beret Guide

House Rules

The problem with playing by your own rules is that reality eventually catches up to you. No person is larger than the world around them. Reality trumps House Rules.

DURING THAT CAMPAIGN, before going AWOL, Custer galloped away from his own column after seeing buffalo on the horizon. He ended up shooting his own horse through the head with his revolver trying to take down one of the beasts.

In 1868, Custer's court-martial was remitted and he rejoined the 7th Cavalry. Under the command of General Sheridan, a winter campaign was planned in order to catch the Native Americans in their camps. During this campaign, Custer's column attacked Chief Black Kettle's village on the

Washita River, even though it was inside a designated Cheyenne Reservation. In this attack were sown more of the seeds of his later disaster.

First, Custer divided his command into four parts to encircle the village. Then he had all the dogs that accompanied the cavalry column muzzled and strangled to prevent them from barking and giving away the advance, even though he could have easily had the dogs leashed out of earshot, indicating a certain brutality of character. Custer then led his men into the village and a massacre ensued—of the Native Americans.

At least those in the village. A patrol from Custer's unit under the command of Major Elliot chased after some Cheyenne up the Washita and were caught in an ambush and wiped out. Custer refused to send aid after Elliot, instead withdrawing his command from the field as quickly as possible under the threat of Native American reinforcements attacking from other villages. This abandonment of his own soldiers earned Custer the enmity of many of the soldiers of the 7th Cavalry and is one of those actions that Custer's superiors should have paid attention to in order to evaluate his character and his ability to command.

One of Elliott's friends, and another officer in the 7th, was Captain Benteen, who would have a role to play years later at the Battle of the Little Big Horn.

Lesson

The best predictor of future behavior is past behavior. 'Good' luck can have disastrous consequences down the line. In combat, such luck can make one believe in their own invulnerability and engender a delusional mindset.

Custer was more lucky than talented. At many junctions

he should have been thrown out of the army (West Point ranking, West Point court-martial, Army court-martial) or killed (numerous charges in the Civil War) that it was by the slimmest of odds he was in command that day in 1876. What Custer considered his good luck turned out to be not so lucky for the men who followed him.

Cascade Two

Custer's ego and ambition.

Custer not only believed himself greater than any situation he was in, he was always seeking greater glory and position.

There is an interesting picture of Custer after the battle of Antietam in 1862. Actually, the picture is of President Lincoln, General George McClellan, and his staff. Custer is in it, but not part of it. It's outdoors, near a tent. Lincoln has his hand on the back of a chair facing McClellan to his right (who by this point, he thought little of). McClellan is facing Lincoln (who, in turn, thought little of Lincoln). The enmity between the two is clear. But it's Custer, off to the right, separate from everyone else, slouched back, hand on the pommel of his cavalry saber that is interesting. He's staring at the camera, ignoring the President and his commanding officer.

WHAT'S LACKING, after studying Custer, is uncovering a sense of duty or loyalty. Custer took actions filtered through the narcissistic lens of: "How will this benefit me?"

He obviously cared little about those he led, based on casualty rates, court martial actions and conduct in battle.

Since at least one cascade event includes the human element, we can see that narcissism and other personality disorders can be a large factor. Often a desire for fame, glory, acknowledgement, etc. are part of the formula for disaster. They lead to poor choices. They also lead to ignoring reality and potential threats.

While Custer would replay his tactics at the Washita eight years later at the Little Big Horn, he also ignored what happened to Captain Fetterman in 1866 at Fort Kearney. Fetterman had boasted, much like Custer's at the start of this section, that he could "ride through the Sioux nation" with just 80 men.

So naturally, on 21 December 1866, when he led a relief party out of the fort, he was in charge of 80 men. He ignored the orders of his commanding officer and marched over a ridge-line and out of sight.

Right into a trap led partly by Crazy Horse who would be present 10 years later at Little Big Horn. Custer knew of Fetterman and what had happened to his command, but Custer felt he was in a different class.

He died just the same.

DUE TO CONVERGING CIRCUMSTANCES, Custer's ego entertained visions of a run for President and ambition can trump common sense.

1876 was the centennial of the United States and a huge celebration was planned in Philadelphia for the 4th of July. It was an election year, with the Democratic Convention to be held in St. Louis, the first time a convention was held west of the Mississippi. With the centennial celebration looming, Custer was feeling pressure to do something significant prior to that event.

Given that Ulysses S. Grant, a former general, was President, elected mainly on his battlefield success during the Civil War, it isn't a stretch to see Custer eyeing the same office due to his battlefield success during the Civil War and now, recently, on the Plains. What if he was the one to crush the Sioux once and for all? So far, three generals who had success in America's wars had become President: Washington, Andrew Jackson, and Grant.

Custer's writings at West Point and afterward show an interest in the Presidency. After the Civil War, and before joining the 7th Cavalry, Custer took a year off from the Army. He considered running for Congress and became very involved in politics. In September 1866, Custer accompanied President Andrew Johnson and General Grant on a

train tour to drum up public support for the President's policies. Many of those cheering were doing so for Grant and
Custer rather than the President.

Just before Little Big Horn, Custer made promises to one
of his scouts, Bloody Knife, about what rewards he would
receive when Custer became the Great Father, aka The
President.

Custer was part of one of three larger columns that were
designed to trap the Sioux in a strategic encirclement. His
orders were to be part of the overall campaign, but left
enough latitude for him to act on his own. Since he'd
already publicly declared his desire to cut loose from Terry's
command, it's no surprise that he decided to attack at the
Little Big Horn, even though delaying a day or so would
have increased the forces that could be brought to bear.

It would also have spread the glory to other comman-
ders, something Custer couldn't abide.

Lesson

The human ego can believe it is stronger than any situation
it finds itself in, but nature, other people, and technology
often don't agree. Ambition blinds people. Looking past an
immediate crisis to larger, and more distant, goals can be
fatal.

When such people are in charge, the effects are multi-
plied. Leadership is a sacred trust and those who are placed
in such positions need to be carefully screened. Ego cannot
trump duty.

Custer was in a rush to not only join battle, but achieve a
great victory. His battle plan was focused more on
preventing the Native Americans from escaping than effectively engaging in a pitched battle. It wasn't enough for

Custer to win, he had to win spectacularly. In Cascade Six, we'll see how Custer divided his command once more, but this time part of the incentive was to keep all the accolades of victory for himself.

He has indeed kept all the 'accolades'.

Cascade Three

Custer's troops were poorly trained and reacted badly under stress.

One of the most fascinating, and least understood, aspects of combat is how many soldiers don't participate, despite being present. There is a difference. The percentage of soldiers who actually fire their weapon at the enemy is surprisingly low.

In the same way, we have little understanding of how people really act in the midst of disasters, as the true circumstances are impossible to reproduce in the lab. We can do computer simulations of plane crashes and building collapses but not of the people involved in them.

For example, one survivor of a plane crash relates how after the plane smashed into the ground, the survivors simply sat there, stunned they had lived through the landing, ignoring the jet fuel seeping down the aisle which would ignite in seconds and kill many of the initial survivors.

The US Army in the 1870s was a refuge for immigrants (many of whom did not speak English), criminals, and the outcasts of society. While the officers were veterans of the Civil War, few of the troops were.

In the Civil War, after a battle, it was common to find many muskets (both abandoned and those from the dead and wounded), which had been reloaded numerous times but never fired. Training held fast as soldiers reloaded, but the actual firing at the enemy was never done.

Custer's men had little experience with their weapons. Because they were inadequately trained, when the battle turned against them, they reacted poorly.

Lesson

Reaction during a disaster is impossible to predict, but training and preparation can mitigate the effect and get people to go against their natural instincts.

In the US Army Ranger School, you're taught to do things you wouldn't normally do. One thing you are trained to deal with is being ambushed.

In Ranger school, the proper response to an ambush is drilled into students day after day, because it goes against your instinct to charge into an ambush. Repetition is the key to this. Do it right every day and eventually it will become the right habit.

Your patrol is walking along a trail and suddenly you are fired upon from the right. Your fear wants you to jump in the convenient ditch to the left—to avoid the ambush.

However, if the ambush is set up correctly—that ditch is mined and YOU'LL DIE if you do that.

In life, avoiding problems by running from them doesn't solve the problem.

Your next fear-driven instinct is to hit the ground. Stay where you're at and do nothing. Except you're in the kill zone and if you stay there, well, YOU'LL GET KILLED.

We all want to ignore problems. Because that's the inherent nature of a problem. But ignoring your greatest problem will keep you in the kill zone and the result is inevitable.

The third thing you want to do is run forward or back on the trail to get out of the kill zone-- escape.

Except, if the ambush is done right, the heaviest weapons are firing on either end of the kill zone. And YOU'LL DIE.

We want to avoid problems by going back to the past or imaging it will get better in the future even if we don't change anything.

The correct solution is the hardest choice because it requires courage: you must conquer your fear, turn right, and assault into the ambushing force. It is the best way to not only survive, but succeed. To tackle problems, you must face them. To prevent disasters, we have to acknowledge their possibility. We have to train to deal with them.

Cascade Four

General Terry offered Custer several Gatling guns (early machineguns) to take along, but Custer turned him down. Custer wasn't so much against the guns themselves, but rather the issue of bringing them along. He felt they would slow him down. Once more, Custer's haste to get into battle cost him.

We must add that machineguns, especially these early, bulky Gatling guns, were defensive weapons, not suited to the offensive. Often, they were carried on pack mules, disassembled. The defense was an anathema to Custer. Even during his final battle, it most likely did not occur to him, until his final moments, that he was being attacked. As a dashing cavalry commander, the offensive was all Custer knew. Thus, bringing weapons designed for something he never conceived of doing, also weighed in his decision.

The military has always been leery of new technology.

While Custer can be faulted for not taking the Gatlings, the reality is that fifty years later, Generals were still clueless about the power of the machinegun, leading to archaic tactics slaughtering millions of soldiers in World War I.

Lesson

Disdain for new technology can have disastrous effect.

Technology is a double-edged sword. In our haste to adopt new technology, we can invite disaster, but we can also do the same by not embracing the advantages technology can bring. In both directions, the key is to study the new technology without prejudice from the past and study how it might apply in an evolving future.

It's said the military is always prepared to fight the last war, not the next. We've already seen that safety regulations are also often rearward looking. As technology advances exponentially, so does the possibility of disasters on larger and larger scales. Also, as systems become more complex, the possibility of cascade events increases.

Cascade Five

Lack of an Area Study and understanding of the environment.

The only glimpse Custer had of the Native Americans encamped next to the Greasy Grass River was from the Crows Nest. While his scouts warned him that the enemy was numerous, all Custer could make out was a milling mass: the Native American herd. One of his scouts, Mitch Bouyer, warned Custer that this was the largest village he'd ever encountered. But Custer was more concerned that the village would disperse before he had a chance to attack.

The fact his scouts immediately began their death chant should have been a warning.

When Union soldiers at Cold Harbor wrote in their journals the date and "I was killed" before the engagement, that should have been an indicator that assault was doomed. Even Grant finally admitted, in his memoirs, that the last assault at Cold Harbor was his greatest mistake.

AN AREA STUDY is studying the terrain and all other factors in a possible scenario, including the history. We'll cover the Area Study later under Seven Ways To Prevent Disasters at the end of this book and in more detail in Appendix A. We've already shown how Custer ignored the lesson of Fetterman which would have been part of a thorough Area Study before setting out on the expedition.

I'd always wondered exactly what happened to Custer. The battle
never made sense to me until I actually went to Little Big Horn.
The moment I saw the terrain, I understood. The terrain can
mask thousands of warriors who wouldn't be seen until the last
moment.

SINCE CUSTER HADN'T DONE a proper Area Study, he was
heading into battle against a force whose size he didn't
know, on terrain he was unfamiliar with.

Lesson

An Area Study is critical to any situation.

We'll discuss this more at the end and it's also covered in
detail in the *Survival Guide* and *The Green Beret Guide to
Success*. It's one of the key planning components for Special
Forces. In every disaster in this book, a better understanding
and appreciation of the environment and situation might
well have prevented the disaster.

Cascade Six

Custer divided his command: making tactical decisions for the wrong reasons.

Custer divided his command into three parts, which greatly aided in facilitating his own massacre. Most people think the 7th Cavalry was wiped out at the Little Big Horn, but in reality, only 5 of the 12 companies were. The rest, under Reno and Benteen, ended up fighting off assaults until the Native Americans retired from the field of battle the following day.

Custer divided his command for several reasons.

One was because his priority was to entrap the Indians and he was concerned they might escape. It didn't seem to occur to him they would stand and fight. Never mind counter-attack.

He wanted the glory of victory for himself. We've already mentioned how one of his key subordinates, Benteen, was not a fan of the colonel because of what had happened at the Washita with Major Elliot. There was also bad blood between Custer and Reno.

He misjudged the tactical field of battle, believing he was outflanking the enemy camp with his own unit, when actually he was attacking directly into it.

It's interesting to note the way Custer broke down his command. The officers of the 7th were a contentious group, half hating Custer, half worshipping the ground he walked on, including his brother Tom, who commanded C Troop. He also had a brother-in-law, his younger brother Boston, and his nephew Autie Reed with him. The companies that Custer took with him were commanded by those who believed in him, while those with whom he did want to share the upcoming glory were sent off away from the battle.

Ultimately, Custer violated one of the 'rules' of combat: Unity of force.

Lesson

One should make decisions based on the real problem, not in hopes of affecting future, unrelated events. Personal conflicts can affect organizational outcomes and produce disaster.

Cascade Seven: Final Event: DISASTER

All five companies and every man that was under Custer's direct command died.

There are conflicting reports on how long the 'last stand' lasted. Based on the overwhelming numbers, probably not very long. Reports from survivors in Reno and Benteen's units indicate firing died out after less than an hour.

It was a Pyrrhic victory for the Native Americans as within a year the Plains Wars were over, and almost all were returned to the reservations. Thus, while Custer was in a rush to get into battle tactically, there might not have been any need for the battle strategically. The inexorable tide of immigrants and fortune-seekers surging west was virtually unstoppable. But it was 1876, the Centennial, and an election year, and the Democratic Convention was being held west of the Mississippi for the first time ever and Custer had visions and . . .

Anheuser-Busch commissioned a lithograph of the battle in 1884. It is wildly inaccurate, but added to the growing legend of Custer. A great contributor to the myth was Custer's widow, Elizabeth 'Libbie' Bacon. After the battle, until the end of her life, she dedicated herself to portraying her husband as larger than life; a fallen hero tragically cut down before his prime.

THUS, defeat is spun into legend and a reckless leader is better known than many others who were true heroes, such as Joshua Chamberlain from the battle of Gettysburg.

From Custer on down through the soldiers of the 7th Cavalry, a lesson to be gained from the 'last stand' is that you can plan for disaster, but you never really know how people are going to react until their lives are truly on the line. There is no doubt Custer was effective in the offensive, when pressing the attack. The defensive, however, was foreign to him.

Despite the warnings of his scouts, and the objections of some of his officers, Custer rode into the valley of the Little Big Horn convinced he was heading toward glory, part of a cascade of events that led to his doom and that of 267 other men.

An organization needs *Cascade Stoppers*. People who can step up and put the brakes on when a leader's ego is driving everyone into an abyss. One of the greatest safety devices in an airplane is a co-pilot who is willing to speak up to the pilot.

Custer needed such a co-pilot.

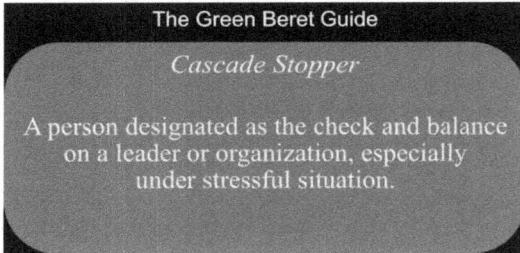

The Green Beret Guide

Cascade Stopper

A person designated as the check and balance on a leader or organization, especially under stressful situation.

Summary

By the time Custer rode down to the Little Big Horn River, the men behind him were doomed. No matter how bravely they fought, there was only going to be one outcome to the battle. None of us wants to be in that situation. The only way to prevent a similar disaster is to catch and stop a man like Custer before he leads people into disaster.

A bad leader is a key ingredient in a disaster that encompassed all those under his/her command.

8

DISASTER 3: THE DONNER PARTY
SOCIAL DISINTEGRATION

"I wish I could cry, but I cannot. If I could forget the tragedy, perhaps I would know how to cry again." Mary Graves. Survivor, the 'Donner Party'

W hen people hear the 'Donner Party', the first thing they think of is cannibalism. That was part of the final event, a result of a number of preventable cascades. By the time this group resorted to that extreme, they had made enough mistakes that we're not going to spend time on that aspect. In the second book in this series, we'll cover another event where cannibalism played a role, Flight 571, the Andes Plane Crash, but that was a very different scenario. The most important aspect of the Donner Party disaster was the social disintegration that led to homicides and the group falling apart because it is an ominous portend of what happens during disasters that needs to be taken into account.

The Donner Party is key because it's a study of group

dynamics or rather, how group dynamics don't work. Few of us understand how quickly the veneer of civilization can be torn away from people. Soldiers who've served in combat zones can attest to this phenomenon, especially among civilians who aren't trained like the military. In locales such as Bosnia, the Middle East, and other places, the barbarity into which apparently 'ordinary' people can quickly descend is frightening. Key to understanding the disaster the Donner Party is that something similar can happen rather easily in future disasters. Turn the power off for a week in a large locale with no relief in sight and the results will be terrifying.

The Facts

In Spring 1846, a group of emigrants departed west for California. Rather than take the usual route, they decided to take a 'shorter' new route, the Hastings Cutoff. The delays from taking that route caused them to reach the last obstacle, the Sierra Nevada Mountains so late in the season that they became trapped by heavy snowfall, and were forced to spend the winter. Starving and freezing, some of the group resorted to cannibalism. Eventually, about half the party was rescued in the Spring of 1847.

The Timeline

1846:

15 April: The core of the party sets out from Springfield, Ohio.

12 May: The party sets out from Independence, Missouri, the start point of western emigration.

18 June: William Russell gives up command of the party,

trading in his wagon for mules to travel faster, along with Edwin Bryant and some others.

27 June: The party arrives at Fort Laramie. They are urged not to take the Hastings Cutoff.

17 July: Passing Independence Rock, the party receives a letter from Hastings saying he will meet them at Fort Bridger and guide them.

18 July: The party crosses the Continental Divide.

19 July: At the Little Sandy River the party splits and the Donner Party heads toward Fort Bridger while the rest stay on the known California Trail.

31 July: The party leaves Fort Bridger to take the Hastings Cutoff. They cross the Wasatch Mountains of Utah, with many delays, taking most of August

30 August: The party sets off across the Great Salt Lake Desert, experiencing more delays

26 September: The party finally rejoins the California Trail at the Humboldt River.

7 October: An elderly man is abandoned by the convoy, left on the side of the trail to die.

13 October: One man decides to cache his wagon; the two men who stay behind to help him, come back without him saying he was killed by Indians.

25 October: A small relief party arrives from California with seven mules of provisions; accompanied by two Native American guides.

November: The party cannot make it over Truckee Pass and camp for the winter.

15 December: The first member of the party dies from malnutrition.

16 December: The strongest members of the party set out on snowshoes to make it through the pass to Sutters Fort (the Forlorn Hope).

21 December: The snowshoers have made it over the pass but are battling deep snow. One member sits down, smokes his pipe, and tells them to go on. He dies.

24 December: The snowshoers can go no further. They draw lots to decide who to kill and eat. But can't kill the loser. Members begin to die.

26 December: They resort to cannibalism.

30 December: The snowshoers run out of human meat. It's suggested they kill the two Native Americans who were part of the resupply party. Warned, the two run off.

1847

9 January: The snowshoers come upon the two weakened and exhausted Native Americans who'd tried to escape. Shoot the two and then eat them.

17 January: The snowshoers are taken in by a Native American village. For the rest of the party on the other side of the mountains, it's uncertain when they resorted to cannibalism of those who died from malnutrition and/or the cold.

19 February: The First Relief makes it over the mountains.

29 April: The last surviving member of the Donner Party arrives at Sutter's Fort.

THE CASCADING EVENTS

Cascade One

The Mexican War.

Lost in this story is an event most Americans have forgotten: the Mexican-American War. Percentage-wise, in terms of casualties, it was the bloodiest war in history for our military.

Technically speaking, the Donner Party was emigrating to Mexico, not another part of the United States. And they were doing so in the midst of a war between the United States and Mexico. I cover this war extensively in *Duty, Honor, County: West Point to Mexico*, so I won't give a history lesson here, but point out how this affected the Donner Party.

In 1846, Mexico technically 'owned' New Mexico, Utah, Nevada, Arizona, California, and most of Colorado. Because of the Texas War of Independence, there was debate about how much of Texas was Texas and how much was Mexico. An explorer named Fremont started a revolt in California in early 1846, in the spirit of the Texas War of Independence.

The Donner Party left Springfield, Illinois for Independence, Missouri, the start point for the California Trail, on 14 April 1846. War with Mexico was proposed by President Polk on 11 May 1846. In essence, the Donner Party was traveling into a war zone.

This factor rarely comes up in the discussions of what happened to the party, but it had to have been something the émigrés discussed as they traveled west. Tangentially, this also had a lot to do with Cascade Two as a push to get Americans to California by certain interested parties influenced the route for emigrants.

Practically speaking, this factor truly came into play on the tail end of this event, when messengers from the desperate party tried to raise rescue expeditions: many of the men who would have participated in these, were off on the coast of California, engaged in the conflict. Fremont was capturing Santa Barbara right when the Donner Party needed to be rescued. This led to a scattered and inadequate response for help.

Lesson

Larger, political events have ramifications that need to be factored in to local, practical endeavors. Deciding the start of a war is the best time to emigrate isn't the best idea.

While there was no law against Americans emigrating to California, the rising tensions throughout the region needed to be considered. This western territory was considered so wide open that the year after the Donner Party left for the west, Brigham Young led the Latter-Day Saints and established Salt Lake City on 24 July 1847, just months after the survivors of the Donner Party were rescued. They did so hoping to be free of the law of the United States. That didn't last long as the end of the Mexican War brought Utah into the fold of the United States.

In an over-arching issue, a country at war has a different sensibility about it. There was essentially no law in those territories outside of the United States. And the attitude of the population during a war is very different than that of peacetime.

Not factoring in the effect a war between the United States and Mexico might have on their journey was just the beginning of a cascade of misjudgments.

Cascade Two

Choosing to follow a new, untried path.

There were two main routes to the west coast at the time of the Donner Party: the Oregon Trail, which was used starting in the 1830s and the California Trail which was brought into service in 1841, but it was still relatively new with a couple of variations.

The journey was considered 'started' at a jumping off point on the Missouri River. For the Donner Party, this was Independence, Missouri. Both established trails initially ran together and crossed the Continental Divide at South Pass in Wyoming before diverging. As you can see in the map, the California Trail in 1846 was still being developed off of the established Oregon Trail.

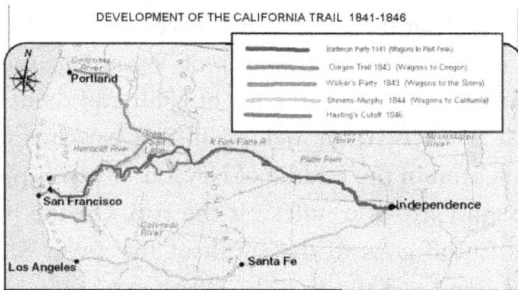

DEVELOPMENT OF THE CALIFORNIA TRAIL 1841-1846

THE AVERAGE JOURNEY took four to six months, requiring a departure in early Spring from the Missouri River in order to make it to the west coast before winter. Regarding 1846, there are two factors to remember: this was before the entire southwestern part of the United States was in the United States; and this was prior to the Gold Rush of 1848-1849. The Donner Party was part of the first wave of emigration west. Even the established trails were nebulous.

Emigration west by wagons was the primary mode of travel until the Transcontinental Railroad opened in 1869. In those decades, it's estimated that 500,000 people traveled across the country. Of those, 10% or roughly 50,000, lost their lives, most from disease.

In essence, this was a very dangerous undertaking.

The Donner Party decided to take something that was new and dangerous, and make it newer and more dangerous.

In 1842, Lansford Hastings wrote a book titled *The Emigrant's Guide To Oregon and California*. You can still get a copy on Amazon. In it, he briefly mentioned a new path to the west, which Hastings claimed was shorter and faster. Technically, on the map, it is. The route broke off from the two older trails at the Little Sandy River and headed to Fort Bridger in the southwest corner of Wyoming, then went through the Wasatch Mountains of Utah and thence across the Great Basin of Utah, before linking back up with the California Trail in the middle of Nevada. It was supposed to shave roughly 350-400 miles off the trip. On the map, the Hastings Cutoff goes to the south of the Great Salt Lake, requiring one to go through the Wasatch Mountain Range, then cross the Great Salt Lake Basin. My experience getting radio calls from the Forward Operating Base ordered me to reposition my unit was that everything looked a lot shorter on the map, than it did on the ground.

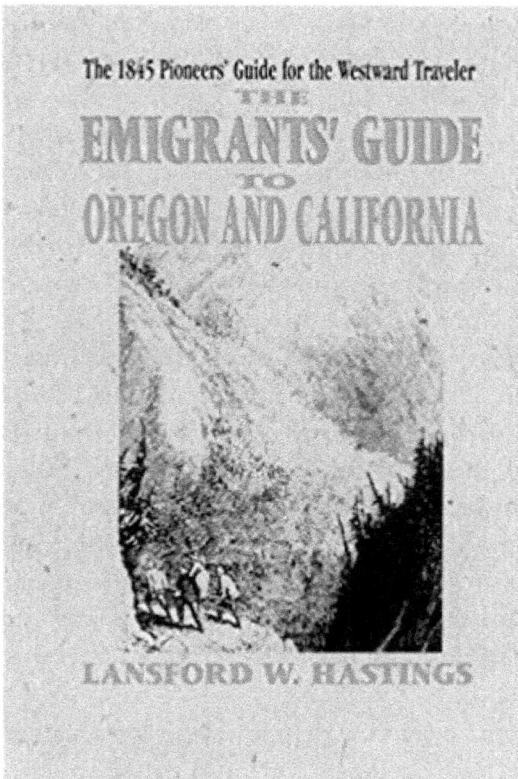

The 1845 Pioneers' Guide for the Westward Traveler

THE EMIGRANTS' GUIDE TO OREGON AND CALIFORNIA

LANSFORD W. HASTINGS

THERE WAS one big problem with the Hastings Cutoff. Hastings had never traveled it until 1846, the year the Donners attempted it. And when Hastings finally did it the first time, he didn't have wagons. Ironically, he did the route the first time, west to east, starting on the same exact day the Donner Party set out from Springfield heading west.

Hastings' motivations were political and financial. One has to remember the people who would make the most money off the Gold Rush weren't the miners, but the people who supplied the miners. Even before gold was discovered, discerning businessmen realized there was profit to be made off those traveling west. Goods were scarce and need was high, always a good combination to raise prices and make money. By diverting emigrants south to Fort Bridger, the owner there, Jim Bridger, could hope to greatly increase a rather lackluster business as his Fort was currently on the way to nowhere unless travelers on the Oregon and California trails diverted south for resupplies.

Hastings had visions of opening his own place at the other end of the line at Sutters Fort, in California. He wrote the book while California was still part of Mexico. His hope was that the book would bring an influx of American settlers to California, which would then result in a revolution against distant Mexico City and establish a new country, in which, Hastings, of course, would be prominent.

One of the early leaders in the Donner Party, James Reed, read Hastings' book and noted the brief mention of the Cutoff.

We're now entering the mindset of the members of the party. Reed was hoping, as many of the emigrants were, to find better financial conditions in the west. He also didn't want his family to suffer overly much on the journey, outfitting them with a double-decker wagon with a built-in stove, cushioned seats, and sleeping bunks. It required eight oxen to pull. His daughter dubbed it "The Pioneer Palace Car."

As the group left Independence, Missouri, they were leaning toward taking the Hastings Cutoff in order to save themselves time and distance. They were also motivated by the idea of getting there ahead of the other emigrants that year in order to find the best available land.

Lesson

We've all been given advice about shortcuts.

The deeper lesson is to always filter advice through motivation and experience.

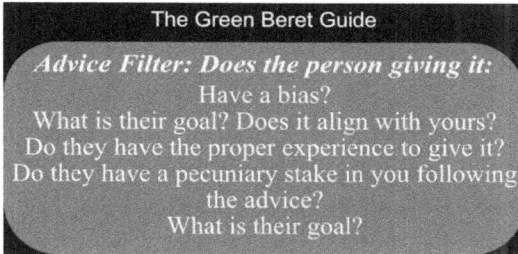

> **The Green Beret Guide**
>
> *Advice Filter: Does the person giving it:*
> Have a bias?
> What is their goal? Does it align with yours?
> Do they have the proper experience to give it?
> Do they have a pecuniary stake in you following the advice?
> What is their goal?

HASTINGS HAD BEEN WEST, but not on the Cutoff. His book did give quite a bit of practical advice and described the country glowingly—reading it, one gets a feel of almost a tourist advertisement for California and a treatise of hatred for the Mexican authorities. But the lack of detail about the Cutoff makes it surprising that one would seize upon it for the journey of a lifetime: By lack of detail, I mean that the entire discussion of the Cutoff in the book consisted of one sentence:

"The most direct route, for the California emigrants, would be to leave the Oregon route, about two hundred miles east from Fort Hall; thence bearing west-southwest, to the Salt Lake; and thence continuing down to the bay of San Francisco, by the route just described." 137-138 Lansford Hastings: The Emigrants' Guide.

The west-southwest direction doesn't focus on the fact that it leads one into the Wasatch Mountains.

While that's not much, the Donner Party would have more contact with Hastings than just the book, as we will shortly see.

The bottom line is that the Donner Party bet its lives on a single sentence in a book read by James Reed.

Cascade Three

Making a bad decision.

Initially, the Donner Party traveled the usual route west. Along the way, on 27 June, at Fort Laramie, Reed met a man coming from California who urged him to not take the Hastings' Cutoff. He told Reed there was a great desert to be crossed and that the Sierras waited on the other side. He further told Reed that even the regular wagon track of the California Trail was difficult enough.

After Fort Laramie, there was still time for the group before they had to make a decision but fate, in the form of Hastings, intervened. Hastings had been giving letters to riders heading east to hand to emigrants who were coming. He warned of opposition to emigration by Mexican authorities in California, advising them to travel in large groups. He also claimed to have worked out a new and better route and would be waiting at Fort Bridger to guide parties west.

The kicker was that Fort Bridger was off the already blazed path to Oregon and California so a decision would have to be made soon.

The Donner Party received one of these letters on the 12th of July.

On The 20th of July, they reached the Little Sandy River in Wyoming and it was time to make a decision. To continue on the main trail or to break off to the southwest toward Fort Bridger.

They made the decision to trust Hastings' letter and route and turned off for Fort Bridger.

Lesson

Between a known and an unknown, the reasons to risk one's life to an unknown must be compelling and trusted.

Despite personal warnings, the party made the decision to trust a man they'd never met. While we might have a vision of these emigrants as hardy pioneers, the reality is they were farmers and business people. For most, this was their first experience in the wilderness. For everyone in the Donner Party, it was their first time in the west. They were threatened by Native Americans, by the war raging ahead of them and, most importantly, by nature.

The only advantage that the Hastings Cutoff gave them was the possibility of saving a week or two of traveling. They were also giving up the safety of numbers as the majority of the party they'd been traveling with opted to stay on the known trail. Thus they paid attention to Hastings about the Cutoff, but ignored his advice about traveling in large parties.

While the party is known to history as the Donner Party, technically he had not been in charge of it to this point. In fact, it had been part of a larger group. And if anyone might be said to be the leader of the group that became the Donner Party, it was James Reed.

But now that they were becoming autonomous, the group was faced with its next decision and made the wrong choice.

Cascade Four

A lack of clear and effective leadership.

After splitting from the others in the larger wagon train, leadership was passed, by group consensus, from Reed to Donner. Reed was former military and older, but his brusque style irritated many in the group. Donner, on the other hand, was easier to get along with. Thus, he was elected.

From here on out, a major problem for the group was a lack of decisiveness in terms of leadership. Decisions were often put to a vote, which works all right in peacetime, but in crisis can often be fatal.

Backing up from this key moment, the leadership of the party was at first sublimated to the larger wagon train. Thus, once they split, the new leaders had little experience.

Here are the leaders the group had since leaving Missouri:

--William Russell, who gave up command when he decided to trade in his wagon for mules after seeing the condition of the trail they were following.

--Ed Bryant, who would send a letter back warning the Donner Party, went with him.

--Lilburn Boggs, a former governor of Missouri, then led the party to Fort Laramie and on to the dividing point at the Little Sandy River, where George Donner was elected. Prior to this time, Reed had been the most forceful and dominant member of their group.

Now the smaller group led by Donner reached Fort Bridger on the 28th of July. Only to find that Hastings had left with a party ahead of them. He had, however left them a note. It instructed them to hurry and catch up.

Edwin Bryant, who had left a week earlier for the west

with Russell, had also sent notes back to Fort Bridger. These warned the Donner Party not to follow, especially as it had so many women and children. Bryant felt the trail was too difficult.

No one in the Donner Party ever saw those Bryant letters. It is debated whether Jim Bridger got them and hid or destroyed them as he had a financial stake in the Hastings Cutoff being successful since it would bring traffic to his outpost.

Instead, Bridger, who had been the first American to see the Great Salt Lake area, told them the Cutoff was a relatively easy journey, free of Native Americans, and would shorten their journey the promised 350 miles. He said water would be plentiful except for a short stretch of desert consisting of a dry lakebed that would take two days to cross.

Even though they got the letter from Hastings telling them to hurry and catch up, they tarried several days at Fort Bridger repairing their gear. Finally, on the 31st of July they left to follow Hastings.

For five days they followed the trail left by Hastings and it was relatively easy. But then they found the going much tougher than Hastings had written and Bridger had said.

They did come across a letter from Hasting on the 6th of August, stuck on a tree, telling them to stop and wait for him to come back and show them a better route.

On a journey where speed was of the essence, with an unknown desert and the known Sierra Nevada Range ahead, the party screeched to a halt.

At this point they did, once more, have options. They were seven days out from Fort Bridger. That meant seven days going back to it. Then they'd have to strike almost due north, a journey of several days, to reclaim the established California trail.

More importantly and pressing, it meant doing the one thing most men hate doing (besides ask directions) and that is admit they'd made the wrong choice back on the 20th of July at the Little Sandy River. It meant losing two weeks of travel time.

So, they waited.

After more than a week with no word from Hastings, and no action on their part, they finally decided to send messengers, including Reed, ahead to see if he could catch up to Hastings. Why this decision wasn't made on day one points to a lack of decisiveness and leadership.

Reed came back days later, at about the same amount of wasted time total that it would have taken them to backtrack and reclaim the California Trail. He had instructions from Hastings to take a different route into the Wasatch Mountains.

This lack of decisiveness, while problematic, wasn't yet fatal. But by not having a strong leader who was clearly in charge, the groundwork was set for the unraveling of the Donner Party as they went further west and things became more difficult.

Another thing to consider is Jim Bridger's advice to the party. While he said it wasn't a hard route, he also said there were no Native Americans to worry about. One has to look at such information from the opposite perspective. If no one lived in the area they were about to travel through, what did that say about the terrain? There must have been some among the party who wondered that. Mrs. Donner thought Hastings a selfish adventurer and wished they'd taken the traditional trail.

Lesson

Instead of Donner making a decision, the group took a vote. In tough situations, democracy is usually not the best course of action (Lewis & Clark took a vote now and then, but they had an entirely different group than the Donner Party).

They elected to follow the new trail. A trail proposed by a man who had twice told them he would meet and guide them and had failed to show up both times. Whose original trail had already shown itself to be much harder than expected.

Now the real troubles began for the Donner Party.

Cascade Five

Crossing the Wasatch and Pilots Peak.

The Donner Party entered the Wasatch Mountains of Utah, with the Great Salt Lake Desert waiting on the other side.

To give you an idea of how difficult the Wasatch are to cross, when I was in the 10th Special Forces Group (Airborne) we were the SF Group which specialized in Winter Warfare. Every year, we deployed for two to three months to conduct training in mountainous, wintery terrain. My first year, we parachuted into the Wasatch Mountains, not far from where the Donner Party crossed, as we were looking for appropriately difficult terrain in which to conduct our training.

WHILE THE DONNER PARTY was pushing through the Wasatch at a snails pace of a mile or two a day, a family caught up with them: the last wagon to leave Independence for the season. This should have been a warning to them that not only was their short cut difficult, it had already turned out to have taken more time than using the regular route.

In the Wasatch Mountain Range in February

ON 20 AUGUST they reached a deceptive place where they could actually see the Great Salt Lake on the other side. It still took another two weeks to get out of the mountains. Along the way, the second member of their party died, from tuberculosis. They'd lost their first member from old age back in Kansas.

Finally, on the next to last day of August they were out of the mountains and at the final spring before they set out across the Great Salt Lake Desert.

They expected to cross it in two days, as per Bridger's advice.

On day 3, the water ran out.

The wheels of the wagons would sink into the desert up the hubs at times.

In 1986 a group in four-wheel drive vehicles tried to cross the Desert along the same route as the Donner's and couldn't make it.

THE GROUP WAS FORCED to detour north to Pilots Peak where there is a spring (you can see Pilots Peak from Interstate 80 to the north, just west of the Utah-Nevada border; there's a rest area with a plaque along the Interstate). They spent a week there, recovering, and searching for missing livestock.

Think of what Russell did all the way back in Wyoming: he traded in his wagon for mules and headed west. At this point, the Donner Party was not willing to let go of their material goods for the sake of speed. They did cache some stuff near Pilots Peak, but they didn't cut themselves loose from their wagons, which held their prized possessions. While they needed the livestock to start their new life in California, they had to get to California first.

When they headed out again, they realized they didn't have enough food to make it all the way, so they sent two men ahead to get to Sutter's Fort in California to purchase food and come back to meet them.

Finally, on 26 Sept they caught up to the traditional California Trail at the Humboldt River. Of course, they were now the *last* group on the trail so they could not trade with another wagon train for supplies.

On 5 October a fight broke out between Reed and a teamster. Reed killed the man with his knife. The group considered hanging him, but then banished him.

While Reed had pushed for the Hastings Cutoff, he was still the most forceful leader the group had if they needed one in a crisis.

Now he was gone.

Lesson

An unwillingness to accept the reality of the situation, even while the clock was running, kept the group mired in a bad situation. Remember that early on, one leader of the group traded in his wagon for mules in order to move more quickly. Yet, the Donner Party, after struggling through the Wasatch Mountains and barely surviving the crossing of the Great Salt Lake Desert, was still focused on quality of life, rather than life itself.

There comes a time during a long, drawn-out series of cascade events, where one has to accept *sunk cost*, and cut loose from possessions in order to save one's life.

Sunk cost is a past cost that has already been incurred and cannot be recovered. It should not be a factor in current decision-making.

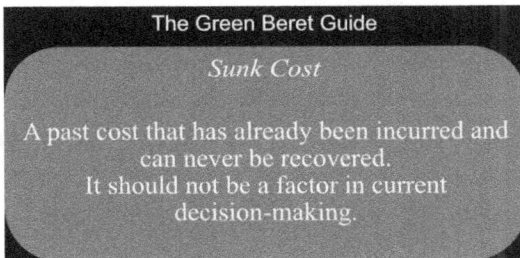

> **The Green Beret Guide**
>
> *Sunk Cost*
>
> A past cost that has already been incurred and can never be recovered.
> It should not be a factor in current decision-making.

Cascade Six

The moment of crisis, also known as the tipping point.

There is often a key moment in cascade events, both large and small, where something happens that indicates future cascade events will be negative leading to an inevitable final event. Usually, this cascade event involves a no-do-over event.

In Erik Larson's book about pre-war Germany, In The Garden of Beasts, *he describes many of the events building up to World War II. While many people point to Kristallnacht (Night of the Broken Glass) in 1938 as the key event signaling Hitler's intentions, Larson's book discusses an event which I believe was the true tipping point, four years earlier. The Night of the Long Knives at the end of June 1934 was when Hitler made his move against the SA. Over 85 people were murdered.*

The key here, the tipping point, wasn't the murders, but the fact Hitler and the SS got away with them. Once they had that power of life and death and there was no force in Germany that could challenge them, the rest was inevitable.

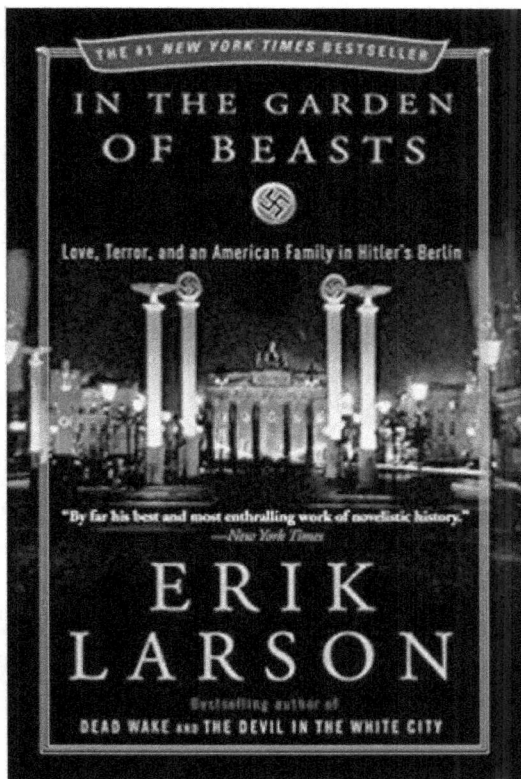

THE TIPPING POINT for the Donner Party came on 7 October 1846. As they moved toward the Sierra Nevada's along the Humboldt River, with worn out animals, everyone who could had to get off the wagons and walk. One of the men owning a wagon forced an elderly man, Hardkoop, who had been traveling with him, out of his wagon. Hardkoop tried walking on severely swollen feet. Unable to keep up, he limped along, pleading with every wagon for someone to take him in.

No one did.

Hardkoop sat down under a large bush, pleading still.

They left him behind.

This meant the Donner party had no leader and was no longer a cohesive group. It was everyone for themselves. And that led to what would happen in the Sierra Nevada Mountains.

Cascade Seven: Final Event: DISASTER

Starvations, freezing, homicide, and cannibalism.

Four days after leaving Hardkoop behind, the group was raided by Paiute Indians who killed and stole livestock.

One man decided to cache his wagon, and two others volunteered to help him. When those two returned to the column, there was no sign of the man who'd left his wagon. Later, one of the men would confess to murdering him. In essence, this was the second murder of the Donner Party: leaving Hardkoop behind was a collective murder.

From there on, as the party went uphill into the mountains, things went downhill. Even though they received a party coming back from Sutters Fort with seven mules of supplies, the weather turned on them.

One thousand feet from the summit of Truckee Pass, while they were camped, it began to snow. The next day when they tried to press forward, they couldn't make it over the pass in snow five feet deep.

During a mission I was on, my A-Team was choppered in to a landing zone. On one side of a mountain range. Our target was on the other side. We moved out. The weather turned and it began to snow. By the time we got close to the summit of the range, the snow was about five feet deep. We had to walk single file, with the front man 'breaking' a path through the snow for six steps, then he stood to the side and the next man took lead. We rotated point for the entire route every six steps. We were carrying well over 100 pounds of gear, but didn't have women, children, and wagons with us. We made it through, but it was the most difficult cross-country movement I've ever made.

We learned in winter warfare that everything takes twice as long as you think it will. Fire and water are the two essentials, then food. The Donner Party was not trained to survive in the wilderness, never mind wilderness combined with winter.

IN NOVEMBER the party decided to camp for the winter, even though they didn't have sufficient supplies to make it through. Their hope was that a rescue party would come from Sutters Fort. The Mexican War probably seemed very far away to them, but most of the men who would have formed a rescue party were away fighting.

Curiously, most made their camp near Truckee Lake, which had not frozen over yet and had trout in it. But none of them tried fishing.

A 16-year-old boy had survived in the same spot the previous winter, staying alive by trapping, but no one in the Donner Party set traps. (In my *Green Beret Survival Guide* I point out that trapping is a far more efficient way of gathering food than hunting).

At Sutters Fort, there was awareness the party was trapped in the mountains, but attempts to raise a rescue party were feeble because most men were along the coast fighting in the Mexican War. The war in California didn't effectively end until 10 January 1847 when US Marines took Los Angeles.

Meanwhile members of the Donner party started dying.

The already fragmented group turned on each other. People bartered for food, selling anything of value. There was no sense of teamwork and certain families hoarded what they had, unwilling to share.

We often see the great sense of community that develops after a disaster such as an earthquake or tornado or hurricane, but most of us have not experienced what happens to a group of people stuck in an extended disaster with little hope of outside assistance. The better angels of our nature tend not to unfurl their wings. In fact, sadly, it is often the most ruthless who succeed, a factor I discuss under team-building in the Survival Guide.

On the 16th of December a group of 17 of the strongest of the party tried to make it across the summit on improvised snowshoes. Parents left behind their children in some cases.

This party was later called the 'Forlorn Hope'. This is a term known to military historians. In the days of muzzle loading weapons, a forlorn hope was a unit of volunteers who led the way in an attack on a defended position, often through a breach in the wall, where the probability of casualties was high. The French equivalent is Les Enfant Perdus, or the Lost Children. The goal was for the forlorn hope to get a foothold, and then subsequent attackers could swarm through the breach while the defenders were reloading. This snowshoe party's goal, besides reaching the other side and civilization, was to get rescuers to come back.

Most of those in this snowshoe group soon became snow-blind a condition most probably weren't of nor tried to prevent. One man simply gave up, sitting down in the snow, smoking his pipe, and was never seen again. They did make it over the summit, but the going on the other side was just as hard.

Stopping, they discussed killing one of their own and eating that person. They drew lots, but no one could steel themselves to kill the loser. A plot was hatched to kill two Native Americans who'd been part of the small group bringing supplies to the party. Warned, the two ran off. But the party caught up to them, lying exhausted in the snow. A member of the party shot the two and then they were butchered and eaten. A double homicide of men who had brought aid.

The snowshoe party lost the trail. What little rations they had ran out. They sat in a circle around a fire, but the wind blew the fire out. Then they crowded together, pulling what blankets they had over the group.

*Here is an excerpt from **The Green Beret Guide to Success** about a lesson I learned during training. It's more about the right mindset for survival than starting a fire:*

I had a moment of enlightenment in the Special Forces Qualification course. During a Phase One patrolling exercise, we spent several days being rained on in February, not exactly the most comfortable experience. Several students had to be medevaced for hypothermia. When the exercise was over, we were given an eight-hour break, still out in the middle of the woods, before moving on to the next training exercise. We no longer had to be tactical.

It was still pouring and cold. Most students huddled, shivering and sopping wet, underneath their ponchos. I watched, though, as one student ignored the elements and walked about, soaking wet, gathering firewood. He piled it up, and then worked hard to get a fire started. After quite a bit of effort, he soon had a roaring blaze and a grateful circle of students standing around, warming themselves and drying off. What I realized was that when miserable, don't just hunker down and ignore the environment— take action to make the environment better. Over the years since, that moment of enlightenment has served me well in numerous

more difficult and dangerous situations. Thinking about being
warm and dry while wet and cold did nothing. It required a
decision, followed by a course of action, literally going against the
elements.
I've seen strong men give up, just like the man who sat down and
lit his pipe. When sick, tired, wounded, thirty and/or hungry, it's
very difficult to keep going.

WHAT HAPPENED WAS that I had what I call a Moment of
Enlightenment. This is the first stage of change. I cover all
three steps in detail in Appendix C.

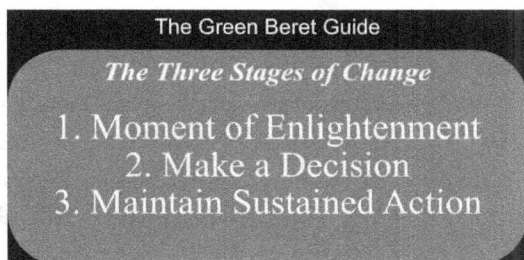

> ### The Green Beret Guide
> #### *The Three Stages of Change*
> 1. Moment of Enlightenment
> 2. Make a Decision
> 3. Maintain Sustained Action

THE DONNER PARTY failed in all stages of change. They
missed several moments of enlightenment as a group
(although there were individuals who spoke out) and they
certainly made many poor decisions or, worse, made no
decision at all. Even when they made it through the first two
stages, they didn't maintain sustained action, movement, at
key moment, including in the Wasatch and at Pilot's Peak.

Many of those in the Donner Party went beyond what

most people are capable of in order to survive, but they'd sealed their fate way back in Wyoming with the decision to take the Hastings Cutoff and then kept it sealed with decision after decision up to this point.

One by one they began to die.

And one by one they were eaten by the others.

History records the rest, a tale of death by starvation and freezing. Resorting to cannibalism. You can find this information elsewhere, because, as you can see, the seeds of this disaster were sown months earlier.

Forty-one died and forty-six survived.

And this all started with one sentence in one book.

Lesson

One has to have the ability to make the hard decision.

Throughout the journey, one gets the feeling the Donner Party was on an inexorable path to disaster. Yet, there were numerous points where a decision could have changed their fate. Whether it be to not take the Hastings Cutoff; to turn back in Utah when Hastings told them to wait; to let go of their extraneous possessions and make the best possible time in order to get across the desert and through the Sierra Nevada's.

The inability to make these earlier decisions led those in the party to make decisions (homicide, cannibalism) that they had never contemplated.

While the weather lowered the final boom on the Donner Party, this disaster shows human error clearly playing a part.

Summary

When I write a novel, there is always one major Moment of Crisis. It's a fight or flee situation for the protagonist. There are also numerous minor moments of crisis in a story. While in fiction the protagonist always fights, sometimes in life, it's better to flee.

The members of the Donner Party had many moments when they had to make a decision. Often, they made it as a group. But each individual, by sublimating to the group's will, also made a decision. And at the end, the group disintegrated.

We all have to watch for tipping points that indicate we've reached a point of no return in the overall situation. Then we are responsible for our decision whether to go along past that tipping point or not.

Between the lack of leadership, the inability to see problems, make decisions, and sustain action, the Donner Party disintegrated and all social cohesion broke down.

Most people who live in first world countries don't understand how quickly the veneer of civilization can be ripped away. When law and order breaks down and people are physically stressed, whether by hunger, the weather, or threat of external elements, they revert to savagery.

9

DISASTER 4: NEW LONDON SCHOOLHOUSE EXPLOSION

LACK OF FOCUS

"I did nothing in my studies, nor in my life, to prepare me for a story of the magnitude of that New London tragedy, nor has any story since that awful day equaled it."
Walter Cronkite

P ropane doesn't smell. It's odorless in its natural state. But if there is a leak, you smell a nasty odor.

Ever wonder why? It wasn't always that way. What caused the changed?

It would have been fortuitous if this had been done from the start as more and more buildings began to use propane and gas for heating. But no one thought of doing it until they realized they had to.

Lessons learned that save lives later, Blood Lessons, often come at high cost.

The Facts

On March 18, 1937, a gas leak was sparked, causing an explosion that killed approximately 293 students and teachers at the New London School in New London, Texas. It is still the deadliest school disaster in U.S. History.

The Timeline

1930: Oil discovered in Rusk County

1932: New London Schoolhouse built; the first in Texas to have a football stadium with electric lights. The school board overrules the architect's recommendation for steam heat, instead installing gas heaters.

1937: Early in the year, the school cancels their natural gas contract and instead taps directly into residue lines from oil derricks.

18 March 1937: Gas that had been leaking in the crawl space under the school explodes.

The Cascading Events

Cascade One

The school board overrode the architect's plan for heating the school.

The original plan, as drawn up by the architect, called for the school to be heated by a boiler and a steam system. But the school board overrode that and insisted on a gas system in order to save money.

The New London Schoolhouse was located in Rusk County and despite the rest of the country being bogged down in the Great Depression, it was one of the richest areas in the country. Oil fueled the local economy. There were 11 derricks located on school grounds. The school was relatively new, having been built in 1932.

Despite a large amount of money spent on the construction, the decision was made to heat the school with 72 gas heaters, rather than the planned centralized boiler and steam system. The architect warned them that the building wasn't designed to vent gas fumes, but they proceeded anyway.

Lesson

Experts are just that.

There are actually two problems here wrapped in one. First, is ignoring the original plans for the building. A heating system is integral to such plans and in this case, the building had been designed for steam heat. Switching to multiple gas heaters ignored the basic construction of the building. And ignoring the warning that the building wasn't designed to vent gas fumes was piled on top of that.

While experts are just that, the Kegworth crash later in this book, demonstrates where experts made a mistake during a crisis. However, this explosion was not a crisis but a planning event, two very different sets of circumstances. Often, during a planning event, experts need to explain why they advocate a certain course of action.

Cascade Two

The school was built on a slope so there was a large dead space underneath it, stretching the entire length of the building.

Add this to cascade one and you begin to see a pattern. Dead space is just that: unused, and often ignored.

Lesson

The term 'dead space' is a misnomer. It's still part of the building. Often, it's places we don't look and inspect that problems can build up over time. Extra effort must be made to periodically inspect 'dead space' in whatever form it takes. Out of sight, out of mind, is a precursor for disaster.

Cascade Three

Eventually, school officials canceled the natural gas contract and tapped directly into a residue line from the oilfields.

This was a relatively common thing in the area as propane was considered waste and usually burned off. A problem with this was that the quality of this gas was of varying quality. Also, they had to run a new line into the gas company's residue line.

This move saved the school $300 a month. While this

might seem overly cheap, remember the environment in the country at the time: the Great Depression was ongoing and the mindset was one of frugality.

Lesson

Cost cutting can be one of the most dangerous things in terms of safety.

It's ironic that one of the richest school districts in the country chose to cut costs this way. But there are two factors playing into this beyond simply saving money.

First, these were oil people. The school's football team was the Wildcats, for 'wildcatter'. Almost everyone there was associated with the oil business in one-way or the other.

The second was that the natural gas residue was there for the taking. One can easily imagine the mindset of a school official seeing the bill they were paying for something that ran right by the school and was burned off and wasted and could be tapped into for free.

Cascade Four

The gas company knew the school, and others, were tapping into the residue lines, but turned a blind eye to it.

After all, many of the people working for the company had children at the school.

After the explosion, during the rescue operations, they found a blackboard with a teacher's note for the day chalked on it: "Oil and natural gas are East Texas' greatest mineral blessings. Without them this school would not be here and none of us would be here learning our lessons."

Lesson

Rules exist for a reason.

The residue gas was of questionable quality and was normally burned off. To allow waste product to be used in the school violated protocol and was a shortcut.

Like cost cutting, shortcuts tend to have negative results.

Additionally, because there was no meter on the gas the school was tapping into, no one could tell if the reading was abnormal. Meter readings are a backup way to tell if there is a leak in the system; if the reading is abnormally large, then there is a problem.

None of the people involved in these decisions and actions had bad intentions. In fact, just the opposite. They were trying to do what they thought was the best course of action.

Cascade Five

The connection to the residue gas line was faulty.

Although no one knows exactly how, since it was destroyed, the line had to have developed a leak. Because of the dead space underneath the length of the school, and the fact it wasn't designed to vent fumes, that large area filled with gas.

Lesson

Cascade events do just that: they cascade.

This was a mechanical failure. They happen. But this failure in conjunction with gas instead of steam heat, dead space, no venting, no meter, and events were now ripe for disaster.

Cascade Six

Students had been complaining about headaches and burning eyes for days.

Since the gas was odorless, the only symptoms were these headaches and burning eyes. It does seem a bit odd that in a community where many people worked in the gas industry, no one took these complaints for what they were.

There were reports that students were in classrooms with the windows open and their jackets on. It's obvious then that people were aware there was something wrong, but with 72 separate heating units, it would have been easy to ascribe it as a localized problem.

Lesson

Paying attention to the details and then taking action.

In retrospect, even with everything else that went wrong, the physical symptoms were a glaring warning. One of the issues with cascade events is focus. To not just notice a problem, but to focus on it and then not assume it's just going to go away.

I've been guilty of this many times: noticing something isn't quite right, but having what I call a *self-correcting mindset*. This is where I shrug off a physical symptom or an anomaly in my environment and just assume it will get better or isn't important.

Inevitably, it doesn't without some action being taken.

> ### The Green Beret Guide
>
> *Self-Correcting Mindset*
>
> We shrug off a physical symptom or an anomaly in our environment and assume it will fix itself.

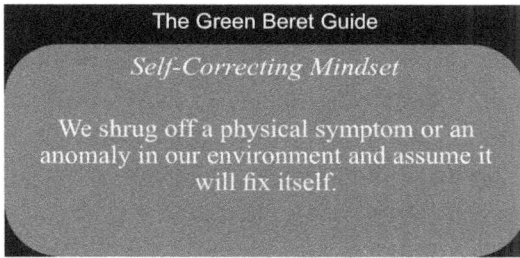

Cascade Seven: Final Event: DISASTER

A few minutes prior to school being let out, at 3:17 PM, a teacher turned on an electric sander. This caused a spark that sent an arc into the enclosed space where the gas had been building up.

Witnesses say it appeared that the entire building seemed to lift up off the ground and then slam back down. People over four miles away heard the explosion and it was felt for dozens of miles. As an indicator of the force of the explosion, a two-ton slab of concrete was thrown 200 feet away from the building.

Fortunately, the lower grades had already been dismissed for the day. The high school was still in session with about 800 students, but many were not in the building as they were preparing for a sporting event. The exact death toll was never fixed, but is roughly around 300.

Walter Cronkite, on one of his first assignments working for United Press in Dallas, rushed to the school. What he saw caused him to make the quote at the beginning of this section years later, even after covering wars and other disasters: "I did nothing in my studies nor in my life to prepare me for a story of the magnitude of that New London tragedy, nor has any story since that awful day equaled it."

Classes were resumed within a few weeks of the tragedy.

The school was rebuilt within two years; this time with steam heat. The loss was so devastating that those who lived there hardly ever mentioned it again. "If you don't talk about it, maybe it's going to go away. Of course, we know it doesn't." (Miles Toler, VOA News, http://goo.gl/ITfQ2l). There is a museum now, opened in 1998. It contains telegrams of sympathy, one even from Adolf Hitler; an indication of how far the repercussions of this event spread.

Lesson

There was one major result of this horrific tragedy, which has undoubtedly saved many lives since the event. Less than two months afterward, the Texas Legislature passed a law which required refineries to add a smell to natural gas. Roughly 1.5 pounds of ethyl-mercaptan per 10,000 gallons of propane is the norm. Thus, since propane is heavier than air, any leak will have a lingering odor that is unmistakable.

However, regarding the other cascade events, nothing much was done. The Court of Inquiry noted the design flaw, the swapping out of steam for the gas heaters, the switch to the residue line, the lack of action on the student complaints of headaches and burning eyes, but ultimately held no one accountable. Some families filed lawsuits against the school district, but the cases were dismissed and never came to trial. No individual was ever held liable and no fine was levied.

The official report said that school officials were "*average individuals, ignorant or indifferent to the need for precautionary measures, where they cannot, in their lack of knowledge, visualize a danger or a hazard.*" (Court of Inquiry, 1937.)

There can hardly be a better way to sum up the purpose of this book than to correct this line.

Summary

This tragedy was the result of well-intentioned people making a mistake. The mistake was compounded by cascade events, as all disasters are.

The most significant problem was never focusing on some of the cascade events, particularly the physical complaints of the students and teachers. Disasters often signal that they are pending in ways we can literally feel, but if we don't focus on those feelings, we don't appreciate the warning.

10

DISASTER 5: THE HOUSING BUBBLE

GREED OVERWHELMS REALITY

This is was taken from Wikimedia and is a direct quote regarding the image about the Tulip Bubble:

"Monkeys in contemporary 17th century Dutch dress are shown dealing in tulips. A satirical commentary on speculators during the time of Tulip Mania, an economic bubble that centered around rare tulip bulbs. At left, one monkey points to flowering tulips while another holds up a tulip and a moneybag. Bulbs are weighed, money is counted, a lavish business dinner is enjoyed. The monkey at left has a list of rare tulips, his sword denotes upper class status. Farther back, a monkey sits like a nobleman astride a horse. One in mid-foreground draws up a bill of sale; the owl on his shoulder symbolizes foolishness and ignobility. Brueghel is not only ridiculing tulip speculators as brainless monkeys, the work is an object lesson for the folly of speculating to such an extent in such a transient thing as a mere bloom. In the denouement at right, a monkey urinates on the now worthless tulips; fellow speculators in debt are brought before the

magistrate or weep in the dock. A frustrated buyer brandishes his fists, while at the back right a speculator is carried to his grave." Jan Brueghel the Younger, Satire on Tulip Mania, c. 1640.jpg. For more information on this image please visit Wikimedia Commons: http://goo.gl/RD8Ued

"W*e never thought it would happen to us.*" Many who lost their houses when the housing bubble burst.

DISASTERS CAN HAPPEN in the oddest of venues and the actual damage can spread far beyond the immediate problem.

Researchers believe that the housing bubble bursting, followed by the resulting economic downturn, had a tremendous effect on the mental health of people in America and Europe. There were approximately an additional 1,500 deaths from suicide each year after 2008. While we can't directly link all these suicides to economic issues, there is no doubt the toll was high not only with suicides but on overall mental health. Many people lost their houses, their jobs, and this stress led to poor mental and physical health.

For the economy, the housing bubble made the dot-com bubble look a bit soothing. Estimates vary, but the dot-com bubble in 2000 lost about 1.3 trillion dollars. Much of that was in stock, which many lower income people didn't invest. The housing bubble cost around 6 trillion, much of that focused on the middle and lower classes. And the housing bubble led to the Great Recession.

Some may feel that an event like the housing bubble was beyond the control of any person and even any agency to prevent. I submit this is a case where each individual could have made choices to keep themselves out of a looming disaster if they had taken the time to look at the events that were cascading over the course of several years portending the disaster that finally did arrive when the bubble burst.

Every one of you reading this book knows someone who was greatly affected by the housing bubble bursting and the subsequent economic downturn. You were affected, as our economy still hasn't recovered from it. Worse, it was those lower on the income scales who were more greatly affected than the wealthy. Losses in the equity of their house and going 'underwater' consumed a greater percentage of their wealth. The wealthy, overall, have a much lower percentage of their worth in their mortgage (if they have one) because it's a lower percentage of their overall value.

What's important about this disaster is that events like it have happened before (like the Tulip Bubble) and they will happen again. It is only through understanding and recognizing the cascade events and particularly the psychology that fuels them, that individuals and organizations can avoid being caught up in a future bubble.

The Facts

The housing bubble occurred in 2006 through 2008 as housing prices peaked and then began to drop. There is no consensus on an exact cause of the bubble, but the focus here is on how the individual can see the bigger picture and avoid being part of something similar in the future.

THE TIMELINE of the Housing Bubble

1938-1939: New Deal enacts laws encouraging home ownership.

1938: Fannie Mae is founded.

1968: Fannie Mae debt is taken off the government books.

1980: Depository Institutions and Monetary Control Act allows more institutions to make loans and loosens regulatory supervision.

July 1997: Taxpayer Relief Act changes exclusion rule for capital gains to $500,000 married; $250,000 single.

March 2000: Dotcom bubbles bursts.

November 2000: Fannie Mae dedicates 50% of its business to low and moderate-income families.

2001: The Fed drops rate from 6.5% to 1.75%.

2003: Fannie Mae and Freddie Mac buy $81 billion in subprime securities.

2004: US home ownership peaks.

2007: The bubble bursts.

THE CASCADING EVENTS

Cascade One

Tulip Mania foreshadowed every bubble that followed.

Tulip mania occurred in Holland between the years 1634 to 1637. Tulips were considered a luxury item and coveted. Speculators entered the market and increased trading on tulip bulbs began to increase the price. Curiously, many of the speculators never even handled a tulip bulb. Or received shipment of one. In essence, they were buying and selling the concept of owning the bulbs. It was called *windhandel* (wind trade) because nothing tangible was being traded. Other than the money.

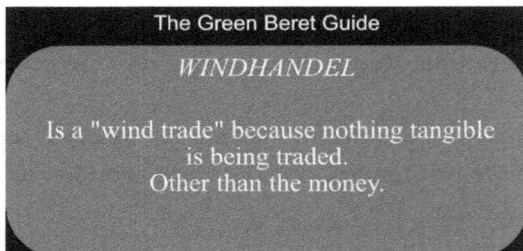

The Green Beret Guide

WINDHANDEL

Is a "wind trade" because nothing tangible is being traded.
Other than the money.

THIS SPECULATING BECAME INCREASINGLY frenzied as the prices skyrocketed. At the peak, ownership in bulbs could change as many as ten times in a day. And often this speculation was on bulbs that had yet to be grown since the growing season was only a few months long.

Prices went up over 20 times their original. People began valuing the bulbs not for what they were, but for what they represented: the potential to quickly make great wealth.

People who had never even seen a tulip, never mind bought one before, leapt into the fray. Fortunes were made, and lost, overnight.

Then one day, no one bought.

And the whole thing came crashing down.

Lesson

History repeats itself and is a great teacher. But delusional thinking leads us to believe that this time it will be different. Rational minds knew the price of tulip bulbs couldn't keep going up, especially at the unbelievable rate that they did. But people speculated on them, staking their life fortunes on the market, never believing that *this* day would be the day the price increases would stop.

Sound familiar?

Not only did prices stop going up, in a matter of days they plummeted, leaving many of those actually holding the bulbs holding pretty much nothing. The resulting depression in Holland affected not only those involved in the trading, but the entire economy.

Something is only worth what people think it's worth.

And thinking can change in an instant.

Interestingly, some modern economists dismiss this event as being overblown and confined to just a handful of speculators. Not surprisingly, some of these same economists are also ones who tended to dismiss the growing housing bubble.

One might wonder how an event centuries earlier can be a cascade event, but before the Tulip Bubble and after, there have been many economic bubbles. What's key is understanding that the housing bubble was not a stand-alone phenomenon. Something similar will happen again.

Cascade Two

Deregulation and tax policy.

In 1997 the tax code was changed so that people selling a house at a profit could shelter $500,000 for couples and $250,000 for singles from capital gains tax. This began to change the mindset of owning a home from a place to live in to an asset to invest one's savings in and then make a profit without paying capital gains.

Starting in the 1980s, Congress began to remove regulations from banks. In essence trusting the better natures of those in the industry, which by itself is such a naïve concept as to be rather stunning to contemplate, never mind actually do.

VARIOUS ACTS ALLOWED BANKS TO:
    offer adjustable rate mortgages (ARMs)
    banks to merge and set interest rates
    commercial and investment banks to merge

FOR PEOPLE LOOKING to buy homes, the ARMs and equity notes were the key factor. Especially when combined later with Cascade Number 5.

Lesson

Trusting for-profit organizations to self-police is naïve.

Congress was influenced by lobbies for the very organizations that laws were made to police. That these organizations failed to stop themselves, even after they became aware of the dangerous path they were on, is because individuals inside those organizations were like the tulip traders: they believed there was great profit to be made even if they knew it was unsustainable. Their irrationality was that as long as that day wasn't *today*, they were good to go.

Inevitably, in every bubble, the day comes.

A desire to make money often pushes people to do things they wouldn't ordinarily do. When NASA shifted from its own schedule to that of its customers (*Challenger* in book two), the pressure to keep to a launch schedule increased. When the radio operator of the *Titanic* focused on his pile of messages to be sent to NY and told the *Californian* to shut up, it had unforeseen consequences.

Cascade Three

The desire for ownership among Americans reached an irrational high.

It is part, perhaps the largest part, of the American dream to own a home (going to college is another one and the student loan bubble is growing and crippling an entire generation). With no-income verified loans becoming common and when sub-prime loans and low initial rate ARMs became available, many who really couldn't afford a house now saw that their dream was within their grasp.

At the moment.

Home ownership rose more than 5% from a relatively steady percentage to an all-time peak in 2004. One has to wonder what made that 5% difference?

No one wanted to look at a prospective customer back then and say: *No, you really shouldn't take out this note based on your income. You won't be able to pay it if the ARM goes up* (and it will go up).

Lesson

It's very difficult to deny people something they very much want emotionally. A logical argument often withers under the desire of want. Desire leads people to make irrational decisions.

A fascinating aspect of this was the lack of a disaster mindset by the vast majority of the people buying homes. An HBO Special *Hard Times: Lost On Long Island* covered some of this, tracking people who'd lost everything. While it focused on the economic impact for those out of work, many of those featured had lost, or were in the process of losing, their homes. And the constant refrain was: "*We never thought it would happen to us.*"

It's rather amazing how people don't think about the possibility of bad things happening to them. Especially when they are taking a risk. We'll discuss this attitude as one of the seven keys to preventing disaster: having a preparation mindset.

Cascade Four

Homes were considered an investment rather than a place to live.

For a generation after World War II, homes were viewed primarily as a place to live, gain equity, and eventually pay off the 30-year mortgage around the time retirement came around.

With the combination of low interest rates, ARMs, and the enticement of no capital gains upon resale, many saw the housing market as an excellent alternative to the stock market and homes as commodities to be flipped rapidly.

Add in that the price of houses continued to rise over the first half of the first decade of the 21st century, and it was hard for people to resist jumping in. Much like people had a hard time not buying tulip bulbs. A major difference is, of course, that a house is a much more tangible and useful product. The problem lay with people who could not afford to keep the house long term, but were looking to flip; also, with people who never considered that interest rates had to inevitably go back up on their ARM.

Lesson

Motivation for action is a key factor to consider. Pretty much every get rich scheme is just that: a scheme. One should enter into them with trepidation and always have an exit plan.

Cascade Five

Interest rates were at an all-time low.

What's amazing is that we will toil all day long at our job, trying to make some money, but will not spend an entire day studying the economy to understand how it actually works. People were taking mortgages costing many times their worth and future earnings without reading the fine print.

Interest rates are both a cause and effect. In 1982 rates on Treasury Bills were almost 15 percent. In 1984 mortgage rates were around 14 percent. At the height of the bubble, interest rates were around one tenth of one percent, something not seen since the start of World War II.

Much like this disaster was a cycle of events, so are interest rates. While we might not necessarily need to know the economics behind how interest rates go up and down, we do need to accept they *do* go up and down.

When interest rates pretty much hit rock bottom (and the Fed went below 1 percent) there was only one way for it to go: up. But we denied that reality.

Along with the belief that house prices would continue to increase, we wanted to believe that interest rates wouldn't go up, even though history has shown both to be false logic.

Lesson

Math works. So does history.

When something is as low as it can go, it's inevitable it will head in the opposite direction. A mindset that interest rates would stay low pervades the pre-burst time period.

But studying interest rates over decades, one has to realize that they go up, they go down, they go up, they go down. They don't stay in one place indefinitely. Actually, the fact they went down so quickly and so low, should have told people they could do the opposite.

Cascade Six

Mortgages were incredibly easy to obtain and lending policies were very lax.

When the guy painting our house offered to broker a refinance, we knew there was a problem with the banking system. It seemed everyone was representing a bank or other financial institution.

Traditionally, mortgages were good bets for lenders as they had the home as collateral. But as home prices increased dramatically, many owners 'cashed out' by taking second mortgages on their home based on the perceived increased value. That was fine as long as the home still had that value.

Mortgage brokers were making a tremendous amount of money, which led them, unregulated as they were, to make as many loans as possible, pocketing the money from each transaction. Many of these brokers had no vested interest in the long-term viability of these loans. Often those giving the loans, especially sub-prime risky ones, packaged and sold the loans, often overseas.

Since these loans weren't on the books of the originators of the loans, they had no incentive to check to see if these loans were viable. The chain of accountability was not just broken, it was buried as mortgages were sold and resold. Some homeowners even had banks trying to foreclose on their home when the bank no longer even held the note.

When house prices stopped rising, things began to get tense. As prices dropped and ARMs went up, people couldn't afford their mortgages. Some went bankrupt, allowing the bank to foreclose, but often the value didn't equal the loan balance, which was a hit on the lender. Others simply walked away from the home. As more and more people defaulted, the lenders began seeing red on their books. We saw a tightening down of lending, not only to consumers but among financial institutions to everyone which helped lead to the Great Recession.

Lesson

The people who became rich during the Gold Rush were the entrepreneurs who supplied the people searching for gold. They had no vested interest in whether those people actually found gold.

I am a big fan of following money. It's the way prosecutors bring down the mob, but it's also the way you can see how someone profits. When engaging with someone who profits in a way that's not directly related to your own profit, you must examine their motives and techniques.

There *were* voices in the wilderness crying out that it was a bubble and it had to burst. Often, doing some research, those voices can be found. What they are saying needs to be checked against logic and the current situation. Often, they make sense. Check them against the advice filter criteria. If they have no vested interest in warning of a bubble, perhaps they should be considered seriously?

Cascade Seven: Final Event: DISASTER

The housing market began to crash in 2007 and continued through 2010 with the Great Recession, and the recovery was spotty at best.

Lesson

Look for warning signs of a bubble in any economic situation. They exist, but our emotions (read greed) often blinds us to them. Victims of Ponzi schemes complain, but they weren't complaining when they were getting returns that made no sense given the current market situation. Then they were smiling.

That's not to say one shouldn't take risks, but there is a thing called a *calculated risk*, where one factors in the possibility of everything going wrong and has a disaster plan. Don't ever be the one standing there saying: *I never thought this would happen to me.*

Always ask yourself: what if the worst in this scenario happens?

The Green Beret Guide

Calculated Risk

When one factors in the possibility of everything going wrong and has a disaster plan in place in case it does.

Summary

Humans will let emotion overwhelm logic. While on Star Trek, Captain Kirk is always more 'correct' than Spock, in the real world, reality tends to win. The signs are always visible before a bubble collapse; the danger lies in not heeding those signs.

Greed often leads to disaster. In the next book, the sinking of the *Sultana* has greed as one of the key Cascade events.

11

DISASTER 6: THE KEGWORTH PLANE CRASH

TRUSTING EXPERTS

Passenger on British Midland Flight 92 reflecting on hearing the pilot announce he was shutting down the right engine: "We were thinking: 'Why is he doing that?' because we saw flame coming out of the left engine. But I was only a bread man. What did I know?"

We put our trust in experts every day. We trust the car we drive will work. The crew of the space shuttle put its trust in the engineers who designed it. A soldier trusts his weapon will fire. Often, we put our trust and our lives directly into the hands of experts, such as when we board an airplane. We trust that the people who designed and built the plane knew what they were doing and did it right. We trust that the mechanics who worked on the plane, did so correctly. And we particularly trust that the pilot is a professional.

We believe that the pilots know what they are doing and are well trained. That they will react properly in emergencies. That we shouldn't interfere with their judgment. After all, what do we know about flying a plane?

Every one of us has been in a situation where we over-rode our common sense in deference to an expert. It can be as simple as a repairman telling us something needs to be fixed, when we really believe they aren't going to fix the right thing. Or that the chef undercooked our meal. But how often do we speak up?

When we put our lives in the hands of experts, and common sense says they are making the wrong decision, it's time to speak up. Even if, as is likely, we're wrong. Because once in a while, they're wrong.

The Facts

On 8 January 1989, a Boeing 737-400 crashed just short of the runway near Kegworth in the UK. 47 people were killed and 74 received serious injuries out of a complement of 126 on board.

Shortly after taking off and passing through 28,300 feet to a cruising altitude of 35,000 feet, a blade detached from the turboprop in the left engine. It resulted in a jolt and a bang. This was followed by a pounding noise, vibration, and smoke coming into the cabin. Several passengers near the rear of the plane noted smoke and sparks coming out of the left engine.

For reasons discussed below, the pilot shut down the plane's right engine-- the wrong engine-- and reduced power to the left engine. The vibration and smoke decreased and they descended to make an emergency landing at East Midland Airport.

Just short of the runway, the vibration and smoke returned as power was increased to the left engine for landing and that engine ceased operating. The crew attempted to restart the right engine using airflow, but because they were getting ready to land, the plane was flying too slow and too low for this to work.

The plane crashed a quarter mile from the edge of the runway.

The Timeline

8 January 1989;

7:52 pm: Flight BD092 takes off from Heathrow en route to Belfast International.

8:05 pm: Flight 092 experiences severe vibration and a smell of fire. Engine #2 is shut down.

8:20 pm: Power is increased to engine #1 at three thousand feet on approach to Midland Airport. At nine hundred feet engine #1 fails.

8:24 pm: Flight 092 crashes a quarter mile short of Midland Airport runway.

The Cascading Events

Cascade One

Engines were upgraded but not thoroughly tested and the pilots were never trained on the upgraded aircraft.

The 737-400 is an upgraded version of the 747. The pilots never had simulator training for the 737-400, even though it was a different version of the aircraft. The first time they faced an emergency in this new model, it was real, not a simulation.

The engines used on the 737-400 were also upgrades.

But since they were modified from an existing engine, inflight testing hadn't been deemed necessary. Lab tests had indicated no problems, so the engine was authorized on the new version of the venerable 737.

A problem was that above 25,000 feet, at a high-power setting, such as when climbing, an abnormal amount of vibration occurred in the redesigned engine. This was not testable in the lab at ground level at the time.

Lesson

Equipment has to be tested in the exact environment in which it supposed to function. And upgrades to an existing piece of equipment must be viewed as essentially making the equipment brand new, requiring all the testing required of such.

After this crash, all 99 737-400s were grounded and the engines modified. One thing you learn from studying plane crashes (besides the Rule of 7) is that almost every safety improvement in aviation has come as a result of a crash, which is a harsh learning curve.

Cascade Two

A blade broke in the left engine.

This is a purely mechanical failure. By itself, it was not a disaster. The 737, and all multi-engine jets, can operate on the other engine.

Of course, this failure was amplified by Cascade One, and, as you will see, became part of the overall fatal Final Event.

Lesson

Mechanical failures will happen. Safety designs and equipment redundancy prepare for this and very rarely do they cause a final event by themselves. This is why we must focus on those Cascade Events that are human caused such as . . .

Cascade Three

The pilots shut down the wrong engine.

As soon as they felt the vibration and received the report that smoke had begun to seep into the cabin, the pilot disengaged the autopilot and asked the copilot which engine was the problem. The copilot replied "It's the le—no, the right one."

There was no fire warning light from either engine, because the problem had not yet reached that stage.

What both pilots failed to realize is that they were relying on out of date data and training. In the version of the 737 they were used to, the left engine supplied air to the cockpit (where there was little smoke) while the right supplied the cabin with air. If it had been the left engine, there would have only been smoke in the cockpit. But since there was smoke in the cabin? Ergo, the smoky air in the cabin had to come from the right engine.

What they hadn't been trained on was that in the upgraded 737-400, the left engine feeds the flight deck and the after cabin, while the right fed the forward cabin.

By itself, this still wasn't critical, but their mistaken assumption was about to get reinforcement. The captain throttled back on the right engine and the vibration and smoke decreased.

Unfortunately, this was just a coincidence. When the

plane went off autopilot they were no longer ascending and fuel was reduced to the left engine. The excess fuel, which had been burning, was gone, and the smoke was reduced. The speed of the blades slowed in that engine and thus the vibration was dampened.

But the pilot connected the reduction of smoke and vibration to his shutting down the right engine. Combining that with what they thought they knew about the airflow via the engines, the decision was made that the right engine was the culprit and shutting it down had been the right course of action.

Lesson

Any time equipment is upgraded or changed; the operators need to be thoroughly trained on all the changes. Even the tiniest change in details can have enormous repercussions. Here, the pilots made their initial estimate of the problem based on a previous version of the plane.

Cascade Four

The shutdown brought erroneous data in terms of reduced smoke and vibration to the crew, who were not trusting their instruments.

There is a gauge, which would have alerted them to the correct engine with the problem from the start. This is the vibration readout for each engine on the video display and it indicated that the left engine was maxed out at 5, thus the source of the problem.

Lesson

Trust instrument readings.

Opening this book, I talked about heuristics and how we often make wrong choices because we base the decision on our experiences rather than real data. Pilots are taught never to trust what they physically feel, but rather always trust their instruments. The reason a pilot can't trust physical input is they don't know whether what they're feeling is coming from gravity or the plane's movement; two very different factors.

Remember ignoring the check engine light? Ignoring the fire alarm? Alarms, gauges, and warnings are put in place for a reason. Feeling abnormal vibration, assuming it was from the engines, wouldn't it have made sense for the pilot or co-pilot to check the engine vibration readouts?

At this point, this plane was well on its way to disaster, but there were still some opportunities for that to be avoided.

Cascade Five

People in the passenger compartment saw the problem in the left engine in terms of sparks and smoke, heard the captain announce shutting down the right engine, but no one reported this disconnect to the cockpit, assuming the experts knew what they were doing. The pilots never asked as they were focused on attacking the problem. However, they had diagnosed the problem incorrectly.

By the time, the pilots realized their error, it was too late.

Pilots in a cockpit don't have a view of the plane. They can see forward, not back.

Lesson

Don't assume experts have all the data or know exactly what they're doing. Don't completely give up control of your environment. Report suspicious data when you see it. An average person seeing, hearing, smelling, noticing something that just doesn't look right, and reporting it has averted many disasters.

To see an engine smoking and sparking, then hearing the pilot saying he's turning off the other engine, it doesn't get any more obvious that someone should have reported the error. Some of those who saw this and said nothing, sadly, paid with their life.

Additionally, it never occurred to anyone in the cockpit to ask the rest of the flight crew in the cabin if they'd seen anything abnormal. A simple call back would have revealed the true problem.

There was a case of another plane in the air where a passenger saw fuel on the wing. He reported it to the flight attendant, who

reported it to the crew. The leak wasn't significant enough yet to register on the cockpit gauges, but there was a leak. The plane turned around and landed safely before that event cascaded.

In the case of terrorist activities, the best defense is an alert populace. The 9-11 hijackers did many suspicious things before the final event. Taking flight lessons where they weren't concerned about learning how to land the plane should have aroused the suspicion of the flight instructors.
But no one reported it.

Cascade Six

The review of data and instruments which might have alerted the crew to the real problem was interrupted by a call from the tower and never resumed.

As per SOP in the event of a malfunction, the pilot had begun to recheck all instruments and decisions as they headed toward the airport. However, before he could complete this, a transmission from the airport they were heading toward gave him flight information for landing. After the transmission, he didn't resume his checks and instead began to descend as per the instructions. It is likely he would have discovered his error in shutting down the wrong engine if he'd continued the checks and seen the vibration meter.

Lesson

SOPs exist for a reason.

Beware interruptions when conducting critical tasks. As we'll see in Seven Ways To Prevent Disasters, SOPs are critical to safety. They've been developed specifically to avoid disasters. When in doubt, a person should stick with what they've been trained to do.

We've all been interrupted in the middle of doing something and then either forgotten to go back to doing it, or missed a step in the process. During cascade events, often we will get interrupted as other things are happening. This can cause us to lose focus. As with many other cascade events, the key here is to maintain focus.

Cascade Seven: Final Event: DISASTER

The plane crashed a quarter mile short of the runway.

They almost made it. For 15 minutes, the plane maintained the glide slope into Midlands Airport. Unfortunately, those 15 minutes of flight were made on an engine that was broken. Engines that are broken and continue to run eventually degrade. More pieces of blades were breaking loose and finally, two miles from the runway, the left engine completely disintegrated, sending pieces flying about. The fire warning light finally came on, and for the first time the pilots realized which engine really had the problem.

This meant, of course, that they still had a good engine; except it wasn't running. This is a case of something going wrong at the worst possible time. If the left engine had blown apart earlier, they would have had more altitude and speed. But two miles from the runway, at landing speed and a low altitude of below 900 feet, the pilots' attempts to 'windmill', using the air flowing through the engine to rotate the blades and start the right engine, failed.

Just before crossing a major highway, the M1, the plane's tail struck the ground, but luckily, the aircraft bounced up, over the highway, and then crashed on the far embankment. It broke into three major sections.

Lesson

Changes were made after this event.

The vibration readouts were made larger and more visible. Crews are encouraged to do more communication between cockpit and cabin during an inflight emergency. Pilots must receive simulator training on any upgraded version of an aircraft.

Since there were so many survivors of this impact, researchers were able to do something unprecedented: examine the position of passengers at the time of impact and their injuries. They found that the crash position promulgated at the time led to severe injuries. This led to the *hands behind head, leaning forward, feet back under the seat as far as possible position* we now see as the industry standard.

The crash occurred very close to a building holding an IBM mainframe that contained a large percentage of Britain's Banking data. If the plane had hit that building, experts realized this data would have been wiped out with no backup. Changes were made to decentralize and backup data.

Summary

While we must put our trust in experts, remember that they are as often wrong as we are. And we know how often we are wrong. Ultimately, they are only human and we are all responsible for responding to our environment and the world around us. When we sense something is wrong, we should take action, even in the face of experts.

12

DISASTER 7: APOLLO 13
SUCCESSFUL FAILURE

"From this day forward, Flight Control will be known by two words: 'Tough' and 'Competent.' Tough means we are forever accountable for what we do or what we fail to do. We will never again compromise our responsibilities. Every time we walk into Mission Control, we will know what we stand for. Competent means we will never take anything for granted. We will never be found short in our knowledge and in our skills. Mission Control will be perfect. When you leave this meeting today you will go to your office and the first thing you will do there is to write 'Tough and Competent' on your blackboards. It will never be erased. Each day when you enter the room these words will remind you of the price paid by Grissom, White, and Chaffee. These words are the price of admission to the ranks of Mission Control." Gene Kranz; the Monday morning after the Apollo 1 disaster; flight director for Apollo 13.

Apollo 13 was a disaster that could have been. While still a failure as far as the intended mission, Apollo 13 shows both the negative and positive side of cascade events working against each other until the balance ultimately tipped to the side that was a hair better.

By all odds, the Apollo 13 mission should have ended with three dead astronauts and the entire space program suspended. Instead it was described, strangely, as "NASA's finest hour." The flight's commander, Lovell, more accurately labeled it: "a successful failure."

As you will see when we go through the cascade events, NASA actually did make a lot of mistakes, but it also did enough things right to nudge out those negative cascade events.

The Facts

On 13 April 1970, on the way to the moon, *Apollo 13* experienced an explosion which crippled the service module and required the three man crew to abandon their moon mission and focus on getting back to Earth alive. Despite the overwhelming odds against them, they made it back to Earth and conducted a successful re-entry.

The Timeline

27 January 1967: A fire in the capsule during a test of *Apollo 1* kills Astronauts Virgil I 'Gus' Grissom, Edward H. White, and Roger B. Chaffee.

.   .   .

1968: Oxygen tank that will eventually be in *Apollo 13* is dropped two inches while being removed.

March 1970: Oxygen tank indicates trouble while being emptied.

11 April 1970: *Apollo 13* launches.

13 April 1970: Oxygen tank explodes.

17 April 1970: Successful splashdown of *Apollo 13*.

THE CASCADING EVENTS

Cascade One

A design change wasn't completely integrated across all equipment.

We saw in the Kegworth crash where a design change in engines wasn't tested adequately. Here, a design change in electricity wasn't factored in correctly to every piece of equipment in the craft.

Originally, the Apollo craft were designed to work on 28 volts of power. However, during testing, it was realized they would need 65 volts to power all systems adequately. NASA directed that all components that relied on electricity be reconfigured for both voltages.

Unfortunately, the company in charge of the liquid oxygen tanks made a tiny error. They refitted every part of the tanks to handle the 65 volts except one thing: a thermostat.

The service module, *Odyssey*, had two tanks of liquid oxygen. Each tank held several hundred pounds of liquid oxygen, essential not only for breathing, but for production of electricity and water. They were so heavily insulated, that they couldn't be inspected on the inside. Each held several pieces of equipment:

- fill and drain valves and piping
- a heater to vaporize the liquid as needed
- a thermostat to protect the heater
- a temperature sensor
- a quantity sensor
- a fan to stir the tank so the amount of liquid in it could be measured

AS PER THE ORIGINAL PLANS, the tanks were set for 28 volts. When the module was upgraded for 65 volts, the thermostats on these two critical pieces of equipment were not upgraded.

As is usually the situation, the tanks worked perfectly, even without the upgrade, on all previous Apollo missions.

Lesson

Once more, an upgrade that affects a system requires intense focus. Double checks, and triple checks need to be done in order to ensure compliance. Issuing a memo is never enough. Compliance needs to be insured by a positive response.

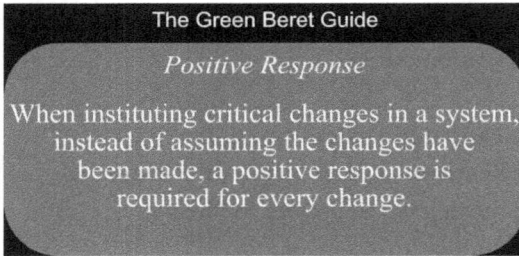

> **The Green Beret Guide**
>
> *Positive Response*
>
> When instituting critical changes in a system, instead of assuming the changes have been made, a positive response is required for every change.

Cascade Two

One of the two tanks was dropped.

The shelf holding the two tanks was originally installed in the *Apollo 10* Service Module. It was removed during maintenance. While this was being done, because a retaining bolt hadn't been taken out, it was dropped approximately two inches, jarring one of the tanks. The tank appeared to be undamaged. In reality, examining later photographs, it was found that one of the filling tubes was damaged and the closeout cap might have hit the fuel cell shelf.

Interestingly, the *Apollo 13* review board considered this incident and the damage as having a low probability of contributing to the accident, which is rather astounding. They were looking for a direct cause, rather than a cascade event. As we proceed further in the cascades you will see how this plays into the next cascades.

Lesson

Any time a critical component is handled in an unsafe manner that could possibly have damaged it, the event needs to be reported and the component checked.

These oxygen tanks were absolutely essential equipment. A chain of accountability needs to be done for such gear. Not just in paperwork, but in personnel. The builder of the tanks, passing them off to NASA, also passed off responsibility. But if NASA wasn't up to speed on what had happened to them, and that they hadn't been refitted, then the responsibility still lay with the manufacturer. Looked good when it left here is a saying in the Field Artillery, indicating that the round looks good when it left the tube; where it lands is another matter.

Cascade Three

Unfocused workmanship.

Two years after the tank had been dropped, something wrong was finally noticed. When the tank needed to be emptied and refilled prior to the *Apollo 13* flight, workers were unable to drain it using the damaged filling tube. Normally they'd pump oxygen into the filling tube and drain the liquid oxygen out of another tube. But when they tried pumping the oxygen in, it just hissed back out at them.

Obviously, something was wrong.

Obviously, someone would try to find out what was wrong with this most critical piece of equipment, right?

Unfortunately, no one did.

Instead of focusing on the issue that something was wrong with the tank, they focused on the immediate problem of getting the liquid oxygen out. Checking to see what was really wrong would have required going through all that insulation and might mean the tank had to be pulled and another brought in. With the April launch window looming, they felt they couldn't afford the delay.

Instead of focusing on the cause of the problem, the workers decided to circumvent the problem and accomplish the task another way: they warmed up the liquid oxygen and vented the gas.

Now the first cascade event comes back into play. A thermostat in the tank was designed to keep the temperature from exceeding 80 degrees Fahrenheit. When the thermostat was activated, since it hadn't been reconfigured for 65 watts, it was fried. The temperature inside the tank continued to rise, reaching an estimated 1,000 degrees Fahrenheit. Well beyond safety parameters.

Since the temperature sensor stopped at 80 degrees, that's what it read, even though the real temperature was over 12 times that. A chart recorder did pick up that the heater wasn't cycling, but no one noticed. What also should have been noted is that a procedure that should have taken days, happened in hours. Once more though, since all the liquid oxygen was gone, the ones doing the job were satisfied they had accomplished it.

The extreme high temperature damaged insulation on the fan power supply wires, leaving some of them exposed. When the tank was refilled with liquid oxygen, a bomb had just been made, simply waiting for power to be sent through the exposed wires in order to set it off.

Lesson

By 'fixing' a problem expediently, instead of trying to figure out what was really wrong, they nearly killed three astronauts.

What happened here is a *system fracture*. Much like a crack appearing in steel or concrete (covered in the next book with the St. Francis Dam failure), it's a harbinger that something is wrong. And will get worse. A system fracture never gets better on its own. When the oxygen couldn't be pumped in, it was apparent the tank wasn't working properly. Every organization needs someone who focuses on fractures and is able to make sure that the problem is dealt with.

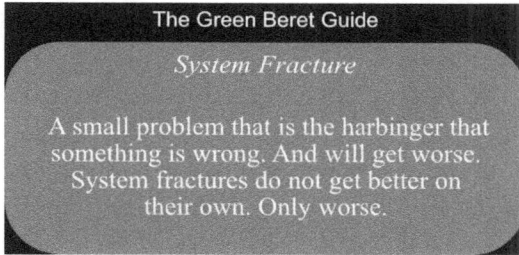

> **The Green Beret Guide**
>
> *System Fracture*
>
> A small problem that is the harbinger that something is wrong. And will get worse. System fractures do not get better on their own. Only worse.

Cascade Four

Mechanical failure. When the fan was turned on to stir the tanks 55 hours and 54 minutes into the flight toward the moon, the oxygen tank exploded.

Actually, Swigert had stirred the tanks twice already, but he had never turned on the heater. When he did, the power flowing to the heater struck a spark in the oxygen rich environment. The tank burst, taking out the other tank and all the spare oxygen and power for both modules. The only power left was that which was in the batteries.

Lesson

A fracture can become an explosion.

What was needed was someone to step up and say: *Obviously this tank is damaged. We don't know the extent of the damage and we cannot, in good conscience, allow it to be placed on that module until we know exactly what's wrong with it.*

Cascade Five

The disaster of *Apollo 1* helped save the astronauts on *Apollo 13*.

Three astronauts died on 27 January 1967 during a test on the launch pad. Fire roared through the *Apollo 1* cabin, killing Gus Grissom, Ed White and Roger Chaffee in the command module.

Since the Apollo program was entering uncharted territory, almost everything that was being designed was unique, particularly the command module. When the first spaceship was delivered to the Kennedy Space Center in 1966 there were 113 significant incomplete planned engineering changes with another 623 change orders made after delivery.

It's a miracle that with that much to be done, that the program succeeded in accomplishing the goal of putting a man on the moon.

One area that concerned the *Apollo 1* crew greatly was the amount of flammable material in the command module, especially since it was going to be an oxygen-rich environment. There was a lot of nylon netting and Velcro scattered about, which was convenient for holding tools, manuals and other equipment, but rather dangerous for those inside if there was ever a fire.

The crew felt so strongly about it, they posed in a parody of their official portrait with all three heads bowed and their hands clasped in prayer. They sent the picture to their project manager saying: "It's not that we don't trust you, Joe (project manager). But this time we've decided to go over your head."

As EVENTS WOULD PROVE, their prayers were in vain.

"You sort of have to put that out of your mind," said Gus Grissom in a December 1966 interview. "There's always a possibility that you can have a catastrophic failure, of course; this can happen on any flight; it can happen on the last one as well as the first one. So, you just plan as best you can to take care of all these eventualities, and you get a well-trained crew and you go fly."

This is the attitude that, overall, made the US Space Program a success and astronauts true heroes.

On 27 January 1967, the crew of *Apollo 1* was going to do a 'plugs out' test. Where the capsule was disconnected from all outside power sources and functioned on internal power alone. This test was key to making the 21 February launch date. It wasn't considered a dangerous test because there was no fuel loaded and all pyrotechnic devices were disabled.

As soon as they were in their suits, and strapped into their seats, the first problem arose. Grissom reported a strange odor in the air in his suit. They shut down the countdown and an air sample was taken. But no cause could be found.

Later, the investigation said this odor had nothing to do with the subsequent fire. I submit it did have something to do, even if it technically didn't. Grissom's sixth sense was picking up something, but neither he, nor anyone else, could figure out what exactly was wrong. As events would prove, something *was* wrong.

Sixth sense is something you can't quantify. I believe sixth sense is the power of the subconscious taking care of us. It is the subconscious picking up signals from the other five senses that we are not consciously aware of, and putting them together, subtly sending a message into our conscious to warn us.

A good point man on a patrol should have excellent sixth sense. His eyes might notice something—a broken twig, a trip wire—that his mind does not really 'see'. i.e. consciously process. The subconscious though, processes this information and sends a warning to the conscious mind in some form.

The Green Beret Guide

Sixth Sense

The subconscious mind picking up real signals from our five senses that we are not consciously aware of, and putting them together to warn us.

UNFORTUNATELY, not finding any problems, the countdown was resumed. While this was happening, the hatch was installed. Here was another potential problem: the hatch consisted of three parts: a removable inner hatch, an outer hatch that was hinged, and an outer shell hatch to protect the capsule from heat during launch and in case of an abort.

When the inner two hatches were sealed, the cabin was filled with pure oxygen at a pressure slightly higher than atmospheric pressure. An issue with the hatches is that the inner hatch opened inward because of the overpressure inside. This meant it would be very hard to remove from the interior in an emergency.

More problems developed during the test.

An alarm went off when oxygen to the spacesuits went too high.

Grissom's mike got stuck in the transmit mode. Grissom grew more and more frustrated with the entire exercise: "How are we going to get to the Moon if we can't talk between three buildings?"

They continued to work through the problems. At 6:30, a voltage jolt was recorded. Ten seconds later Chaffee exclaimed "Hey!" and White announced "I've got a fire in the cockpit!"

Because the cabin was filled with pure oxygen, it burned fast. 17 seconds after the first report of fire, there was a scream and then all transmission ceased. The capsule itself ruptured due to the fire.

It took five minutes to get through the three hatches to the men inside. At the same time, there was fear the capsule would explode and/or the fire might ignite the solid fuel rockets in the launch escape tower.

Once inside, they found the astronauts.

It took over 90 minutes to remove the bodies due to the

large amount of melted nylon that fused them to the capsule.

The cause of the fire was never exactly pinned down but NASA did finally understand that everything inside a capsule pumped full of almost pure oxygen needed to be protected better, especially wiring. They found over 34 square feet of Velcro and 70 pounds of other flammable material in the small space.

In retrospect, NASA realized they had never run a fire test on the command module prior to testing it with people inside. They also realized having a higher pressure inside made removal of the inner hatch impossible.

Lesson

Lessons learned and applied from previous disasters, the gifts of failure, can be used to prevent future disasters.

As a result of the *Apollo 1* fire and the sacrifice of three brave men, NASA fire-proofed all future Apollo capsules with non-flammable materials, switched the atmosphere to a less flammable nitrogen-oxygen mix, and made sure all electrical connections were specially coated.

While an electrical arc did cause the *Apollo 13* explosion, it was inside a tank subcontracted outside of NASA. Senior engineers, after *Apollo 13* made it back, said that if the capsule hadn't been upgraded with all these fire-proof changes, it very likely would have burned up on re-entry, especially since water droplets which condensed from the astronaut's breathing got into almost everything and would have caused arcs.

Cascade Six

Innovation, disaster planning and leadership helped save *Apollo 13*.

After the tank blew, *Apollo 13* was in very bad shape. Three key things stand out in how the flight managed to survive once Cascade Six happened:

ONE: The crew was able to build a box to scrub CO_2 based on innovation by their ground support personnel using the limited supplies available. A master alarm went off, signaling that they had exceeded a safe level of CO_2 and the scrubbers needed to be switched out. Ground personnel were frantically at work trying to devise a way to make the square canisters from Odyssey function in the round adapters on Aquarius.

The first issue here is why did the two craft have different equipment? Standardization is key to redundancy.

Nevertheless, over 100 personnel working on the ground came up with a way to make the square canisters fit into the round system. They ended up using duct tape, plastic bags, space suits and other field expedient ways to make this happen. In the Army we called duct tape "hundred mile an hour tape" because that's how fast it disappeared.

The astronauts built this improvised system, which they christened the 'mailbox' step-by-step following instructions from the ground. By themselves, they most likely would not have been able to innovate this piece of equipment. They needed a team on the ground, working hard, in order to produce the mailbox.

. . .

Two: The remote contingency of using the LEM as a lifeboat had been considered and planned for.

When the full extent of the problem became apparent, it was realized that the LEM, *Aquarius*, had to be used as a lifeboat for the journey back to Earth. The craft wasn't designed for that so they were entering radically new territory, fraught with danger and having to make rapid, life-threatening decisions.

Except they weren't entering uncharted territory. Some engineers at NASA had been working on just this scenario for a while.

A year previously, during the simulations for the *Apollo 10* mission, the flight controllers, in concert with the astronauts, had come up with a scenario where the fuel cells failed—similar to the problem *Apollo 13* was now experiencing. The solution was to use the lunar module as a lifeboat; exactly what they needed to do with *Apollo 13*.

It wasn't easy during the simulation. The people on hand couldn't solve it so help was brought in. Even then, they were unable to get the module powered up in time and the crew "died".

The failure caused most to dismiss it as a possibility because they had been unable to accomplish it. After all, such a scenario envisioned the simultaneous failure of so many systems at the same time, it couldn't possibly happen.

Except it did with *Apollo 13*.

Fortunately for that crew, there were some who were involved in the simulation who couldn't let it go. It bothered some that a crew had "died" even if just in a simulation. A team was tasked with making the solution work, throwing in a crippled command module just to make it tougher.

When *Apollo 13* ran into trouble, what this task force had done was dusted off and implemented, making an impossible situation possible. By the time they got the lunar module on line, it was estimated the crew had barely 15 minutes of oxygen left. Contingency planning is part of disaster planning.

THIRD: One person was in charge on the ground.

There is a difference between management and leadership. In a cascade event, leadership is needed. One person has to make decisions, because time is often of the essence.

At NASA, the flight controller is ultimately responsible for the success of the mission and the lives of the astronauts under their command. Their creed states that they must "always be aware that suddenly and unexpectedly we may find ourselves in a role where our performance has ultimate consequences."

Apollo 13 was one of those times when the flight director was in that role.

Gene Kranz was the flight director in charge when the tank exploded. His mission tasking was: "The flight director may take any action necessary for crew safety and mission success."

Note how mission and crew flip flop in his mission tasking from the creed?

For *Apollo 13*, very quickly, the decision was made that the mission, landing on the moon, had to be scrubbed if there was to be any chance of getting the astronauts back alive.

Kranz made a number of key decisions as a leader, but as importantly he set the tone for the others working in flight control. Immediately after the explosion, Kranz let everyone know how things were going to work: "Okay, let's everybody keep cool. Let's solve the problem, but let's not make it any worse by guessing."

During simulations, NASA had learned that getting too far ahead of the problem could cause decisions to be made that couldn't be unmade. A no-do-over.

Kranz stayed in command until *Apollo 13* made it back safely to Earth. Even when other shifts were on duty, he still had the final word.

Lesson

Innovation, disaster planning before the cascade event and decisive leadership were key to preventing this last cascade event from becoming a final event.

Cascade Seven: Final Event: DISASTER AVERTED

Successful splashdown.

The crew transferred over to the command module and let go of their lifeboat, the lunar module, *Aquarius*. The crew jettisoned the service module as they neared Earth. They took pictures to check the extent of the damage and were surprised at the extent.

The crew was uncertain if their heat shield had been damaged during the explosion, but at this point, they had no choice. They had to re-enter.

Normal blackout for re-entry was four minutes. *Apollo 13's* lasted a very anxious 87 second longer than that, but they made splashdown in the Pacific safely.

Lesson

During re-entry, it is believed the capsule would have had an internal fire if the lessons learned from the fire inside *Apollo 1's* capsule.

Summary

Apollo 13 failed in its mission. But it avoided being a disaster due to leadership, innovation under stress and disaster planning.

13

SEVEN WAYS TO PREVENT DISASTERS

Have A Preparation Mindset

The key is to accept that shit doesn't just happen. As you now know, most disasters are the result of cascade events. The origins of future disasters lie in our past and in our present.

When my A-Team traveled, my engineers would always be looking at things they saw with a different perspective than most people. When they saw a bridge, they were mentally calculating how to blow it up. When they saw a stream, they were thinking how to dam it and provide a water supply to villagers. My weapons men would look at terrain for fields of fire. To be a survivor, you have to look at your environment in terms of what you can use and what can be a threat, which requires you to assume a different mindset.

THE BEST WAY TO prevent a disaster is to plan for it. If engineers at NASA had not planned for the unlikely 'lifeboat' possibility, the crew would have never made it back.

In order to plan for it, you must do the next six things.

Focus

Pay attention, both to immediate events and surroundings, and the past. We generally think in one of two different ways: a big picture thinker or a detail thinker.

Both types are needed. Understand your own predilection for big picture versus detail and for those in your organization. An organization needs both and a way to integrate them to support each other.

A big picture thinker can see patterns. This person can put the pieces together in order to see trends that could lead to disaster.

A big picture thinker would see the flow of history regarding bubbles and have known the housing bubble was inevitable.

Unfortunately, a big picture thinker might miss the key details that make up those trends.

A big picture thinker might have passed over that single sentence in the book about the Hastings Cutoff and focused on the fact the California Trail was the way people had successfully been journeying to California.

A detail thinker would have noticed many of the elements of Cascade Events. Binoculars locked up on a huge ship like the *Titanic* is a pretty small detail at the time, but in retrospect that single event loom large.

For the New London Schoolhouse, some people certainly noted the ill students, but might not have been able to connect that with leaking gas.

For both types, they have to focus hard on the area they are lacking.

I'm a big picture thinker. So, I've had to work very hard to focus on details. I've had to learn not to get upset when a detail is pointed out to me that I haven't noticed. In fact, I've had to learn to focus on what I call an anger indicator. I always advise people

that when they get angry, it's usually because they're hearing or
seeing or experiencing a truth they don't want to.
When I get angry, I always try to focus on what exactly it is that
is making me upset and in doing so I can often uncover key
truths. The more an organization fights something, the more
likely that something is going to be part of a cascade event.
*More on this in **The Green Beret Guide for Success.***

Conduct Area Studies

In Special Forces, prior to deploying to an Area of Operations, we conducted an Area Study of that location. You must conduct an Area Study of your Area of Operations (AO). This is your home, your work, and any other locales where you spend a significant amount of time. When taking a trip, you should conduct a travel area study, examining the route you will take, your destination, and your route back.

There are so many cases where a thoughtful Area Study followed up by the appropriate preparations would have saved lives and avoided disaster. Preparation is so much better than reacting.

Custer certainly would have benefited from an area study. At the very least, a better reconnaissance would have shown him what he was really up against.

The Donner Party put their lives on the line because of the words of a man who had not done an area study, but wrote as if he had.

Think about it. You live in a tsunami zone. Have you actually driven your evacuation route? How long does it take? Have you figured out the quickest escape route on foot, when an accident caused by terrified people blocks the road or everyone in your neighborhood fleeing on the same route creates a traffic jam? You work on the 90th floor of a skyscraper. Do you ever look around and ask yourself: how do I get out of here if the normal means of egress are blocked?

How close are you to the nearest military base? Nearest police station? Firehouse? Hospital? Do you know where the closest emergency room is? How long it will take to get there? How quickly can an ambulance respond to your location?

You want to examine your environment for a lot of things. What can harm you? What can help you? What can hide you? What are your enabling factors? What are your disabling factors? What effect does your environment have on you? What effect will you have on it? In essence, an Area Study requires you to invest the time and energy on research to prevent disasters.

For an A-Team, we conducted the Area Study in Isolation where we were locked up 24/7 in a secure compound. We'd bring in area experts (CIA agents, State Department personnel, people who'd traveled there, locals, academics, etc.) to tell us about the

environment we were heading into. This is a technique I recommend for businesses under my Green Beret Guide program.

GET a HALO study of your environment and organization. This might be the time to bring in an outsider with no preconceived notions of how your business/organization functions. Surprisingly, often in describing things to an outside, or answering questions, you'll realize things you never considered before. We take too many things for granted. "*It's always been done this way*" is never a good reason to keep doing it that way.

An Area Study must combine with the disaster mindset to focus on the possibility that what can go wrong will go wrong!

Appendix A contains more detail about doing an Area Study.

An Area Study should be combined with . . .

Use the CARVER Formula

CARVER is a formula we use in Special Forces to assess targets for specific missions. It is the way we find critical nodes and the places where disaster is most likely to happen; or in our case, be *made* to happen.

You can apply the CARVER Formula to your organization by considering it a target for disaster and then reverse think it. As a novelist, I start a thriller by taking the bad guy's point of view and coming up with his or her nefarious plan. As a disaster preventer, you have to take the point of view opposite to what you're used to: how can my organization, ship, plane, building, business, etc. fall apart? Be destroyed?

By both man-made and natural forces? Once you figure those possibilities out, you can then work to prevent cascade events.

A very recent example: In the very first draft of my survival guide over a decade ago, in the section on pandemics, I wrote "preparing for the inevitable pandemic". The same with the free slideshow I put together: *Prepare for and survive the inevitable pandemic.* Note the word *inevitable.* Which begs the question: how many individuals and organizations were prepared for COVID-19?

HERE IS CARVER, which is a framework you can use:

CRITICALITY: How important is the target? What are the critical nodes of the target? For example, to put a port out of commission for a while, a critical node might be the shipping channel. Or the cranes that load and off-load cargo. Or Pearl Harbor's fuel depot (Book 2 in this series).

ACCESSIBILITY: Can the target be gotten to? How? Can the part of the target that is to be destroyed be accessed? There are often many critical nodes, but some are more easily disrupted than others, thus making it more vulnerable.

RECUPERABILITY: How long will it take to fix the damage done to the target? How quickly can you recover from a cascade event or a final event?

VULNERABILITY: Will the team have the capability to actually destroy the target? For example, a dam requires a tremendous amount of force to breach, normally more than a team could carry in. But to overcome this limitation, a team could use a laser designator to guide bombs or cruise missiles in to a target. Never accept limitations at first—there are usually ways to overcome them. How vulnerable are your critical nodes?

EFFECT: What effect outside of the target itself, will the damage have? For example, a team might have the mission to destroy a bridge that the enemy uses to carry supplies over. But will destroying that bridge have too large a negative effect on the population? If part of your supply chain is disrupted, what effect will it have?

RECOGNIZABILITY: Can the target be recognized? Can the critical nodes be located? For example, oxygen on *Apollo 13* was a critical node.

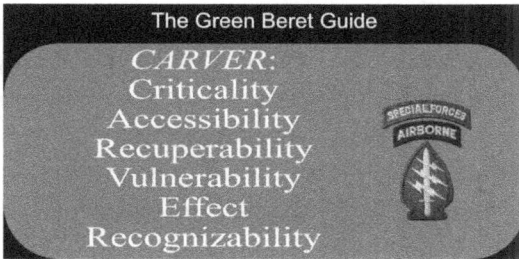

The Green Beret Guide
CARVER:
Criticality
Accessibility
Recuperability
Vulnerability
Effect
Recognizability

CARVER IS a way of looking at the details that make up the big picture.

Have a 10th Man

"When you find yourself on the side of the majority, it is time to pause and reflect." Mark Twain.

When I was watching *World War Z*, one scene really struck me. When the lead character goes to Israel and finds they've already built a wall around Jerusalem to protect themselves from the zombies. He asks how did they know to build the wall before the zombies arrived?

The answer is the 10th Man.

While it is fiction (remember plane attacks on buildings were postulated in fiction well before 9-11), the concept is one that is intriguing for organizations to implement. It can help overcome the inertia of bureaucracy.

After Nine-Eleven, our government brought in thriller writers like myself, to postulate potential terror threats, since it is what we do for a living.

Having been badly surprised during the Yom Kippur War in 1973, the Israeli military has focused on preventing a similar disaster in the future.

In World War Z, the series of events went this way:

Ten days before the zombies spread into Israel, and it was public, the military received a vague email from an Indian general mentioning 'zombies'. Naturally, everyone blew this off. But the 10th Man policy had been enacted where, if 9 people agree, then the 10th man must disagree regardless of how crazy it sounds. In this case, they acted on that disagreement, building a wall for a zombie invasion only one person thought might happen.

The 10th Man concept is an excellent way to build a contrarian point of view into an organization. Instead of being the boy who cried wolf, the 10th Man is *expected* to cry wolf.

But there's more to it than that.

The 10th Man just doesn't disagree; he/she must posit a different take on the situation, along with supporting evidence. This position must be listened to with an open mind. By arguing the 10th Man's points, what often happens is an alternative possibility is uncovered that no one considered. It's a way of war-gaming possible disasters.

A 10th Man in the rear of the plane during Kegworth would have pointed out that the wrong engine had been shut down.

Conduct After Action Reviews

The seven disasters were covered in this book are a form of an After Action Review. The hardest AARs to conduct are when things go well. To incorporate disaster thinking into a successful event.

Also, a key is to focus on any deviation, any potential problem that went away: i.e. a delusion event.

An organization that won't look closely at itself is doomed to keep doing the same things wrong again and again until eventually the events cascade to a disaster.

Because simulated combat exercises are so difficult to observe and judge, the military designed the AAR to help the participants figure out what happened. It was only in the late 90s that the business world began picking up the concept, most likely a result of Army officers filtering into the civilian world and bringing what they had learned with them. The most critical aspect of having an effective AAR is honesty. The first, and most important, question to be answered is, "was the goal or mission accomplished?" Given that your goal or mission should have been stated clearly in one sentence, the answer should be clear.

I have read several business books where it is said an AAR should not judge success or failure. I disagree with that. Why not? The theory is that focusing on success or failure will cause emotional conflict—if that's the case, then so be it. We succeed. We fail. We learn, adjust and move on.

One time when I was jumpmastering, during the pre-jump briefing I forgot to ask an important question: If anyone there hadn't parachuted in a specified amount of time. Everyone participating was Special Ops and experienced so I screwed up by not asking a question in the SOP. It turned out there was a new man in the unit who hadn't jumped in years. Instead of heading out for a jump, he should have been going to jump refresher training. During the AAR, I had to bring up my screw-up even though there hadn't been a problem. The issue was there could have been a problem.

IF YOU ACHIEVED YOUR GOAL, then pat yourself on the back, then see what fine-tuning needs to be done and what potential disasters could occur if things didn't go quite right. Also, focus on any time words like "lucky" or "fortunate" come up.

. . .

STEPS for an effective AAR with a focus on preventing cascade and final events:

--Review your plan. Did you follow your plan? If not, note the exceptions and variations you made. Did any rule breaking of the plan work? What didn't work?

--Summarize the events as they occurred, using a detailed timeline, with no commentary. Just the facts. Build a complete timeline of action.

--Focus on why each specific action was taken. Whether each step of the plan was followed, or deviated from (which is not necessarily a bad thing).

--Give particular focus to when fear played a role in your actions—this is the most difficult part of the AAR, but the most critical—fear is most likely where your actions diverged from your plan.

--Examine what role SOPs played. Did they work? Do they need to be revised? Were SOPs ignored? If so, why?

--Summarize areas of plan improvement and refinement, as well as alternative actions you could have taken to achieve a more successful result.

--What were the lucky breaks during the activity?

--When did you dodge the bullet?

--What if we'd failed? What would have been the critical nodes where failure was most likely? How can we make sure those critical nodes aren't as vulnerable?

THE KEY IS to make hindsight, foresight.

Something to remember is there are over 1,000 near misses for every work accident that results in a serious injury or death. The more focus that is placed on near misses, the less common they become and the less likely a serious injury or death occurs.

After Action Reviews are worthless if they aren't used. They need to be made accessible to everyone and kept on file in a way they can easily be found. Too many organizations reinvent the wheel over and over because they don't learn from their own past. AARs are good ways to begin writing your SOPs.

Use Standing Operating Procedures

Standing Operating Procedures (SOPs) are anything written down that delineates how things should be done. They can serve many purposes. The key part of the first sentence is *written down*. Writing something down makes it real. It also makes it available to everyone. It reduces confusion and misunderstanding. It also clearly designates responsibility.

Every job I've ever done, I've ended up writing an SOP for it. Usually I do this because no one before me did it, even when it was part of their job. I also did it so I could better understand what I was supposed to be doing.

When I finished my Special Forces training at Fort Bragg, I was issued orders assigning me to the 10th Special Forces Group (Airborne) at Ft Devens, MA. I was assigned as a team's executive officer. After being in-briefed by the team leader, he asked me if I had any questions. The first thing I did was ask him for the team's SOP, as I had been taught to do at Fort Bragg. I was surprised when he told me they didn't have one. He had explanations why they didn't need one, but ultimately, in retrospect, the primary reason was no one had taken the initiative to write one, because writing an SOP is a very time-consuming process. It's a 'front-end'-'back-end' deal. You put the work in on the front end to save you considerably more time in the long run on the back end. Unfortunately, too often, people are overwhelmed up front and don't see the larger and long-range picture.

When I took command of my own A-Team, once again, the first thing I asked was where was the team SOP. After my previous experience, I wasn't too surprised when I was told the team didn't have one written down. They 'knew' what they needed to do, I was told. Right. And even if they did, how was I supposed to 'know' it?

So, I began writing the team SOP. Basically, I began formalizing what everyone said they 'knew'. I not only drew from my team members' expertise, I went to other teams and found those who did have SOPs and got copies. I went to the company headquarters and talked to the Sergeant Major who had extensive combat experience and got him to help, giving us some tips—seemingly small, but ones that could save your life in combat.

The team SOP when completed was rather detailed and a living document that we constantly refined as we tested concept sin it and learned what worked and what didn't. The beginning of it was mine and my team sergeant's policy letters, spelling out our philosophy for leading the team.

MY TEAM SERGEANT was direct and to the point. Here were some of his choicer lines:

Nothing is impossible to the man who doesn't have to do it.

Smith & Wesson beats four aces.

The latest information hasn't been put out yet.

There are two types of soldiers— the steely eyed killer and the beady eyed minion.

Here are some excerpts from mine:

Most basic tenet of teamwork is honesty.

With rank & privilege comes responsibility.

Everyone is a leader.

We do everything together.

If you have a problem with someone with higher rank, let me know.

Keep a positive attitude.

Discipline stays at team level.

Be on time.

Keep your sense of humor. You'll need it.

AFTER THE POLICY LETTERS, we then specified who on the team was responsible for what. We took much of this from the field manual for Special Forces that had this information. You can help yourself tremendously when writing an SOP to check out what is already out there. Someone, somewhere, probably wrote one just like what you want to write. It might well be buried in the file cabinets or on a thumb drive somewhere.

We then covered numerous tactical situations and codified how each team member would act. Then we would train on those SOPs until the actions became instinctual.

SOPs Codify And Set Standards

WHEN I WAS FIRST PUBLISHED, I attended a continuing education class on magazine writing. I didn't have plans to write articles, but I figured it was a form of writing so I would learn something. I was trying to get out of my tunnel vision. The instructor gave out a thin comb-bound booklet covering the material he was going to teach. I thought this was a good idea and when I was getting ready to teach my first writing class, I did the same and ended up with *The*

Novel Writers Toolkit. I also learned a lot about the publishing industry from a writer's point of view and wrote *Write It Forward*, an SOP for authors to understand and master the business.

Special Operations has always relied on SOPs. If you get a copy of the current US Army Ranger Handbook, which every good Infantry and Special Forces officer should be packing, in the very beginning is a list of **Roger's Rules of Rangering**. The first Rangers were formed in 1756 and Rogers wrote his rules in 1759 after three years of combat experience on the frontier. Some of these sound quite simple but they were learned, as many of the lessons in this book were, at the cost of blood:

Don't forget nothing.

Tell the truth about what you see and do.

When you're on the march, act the way you would if you were sneaking up on a deer. See the enemy first.

Don't never take a chance you don't have to.

When we camp, half the party stays awake while the other half sleeps.

Don't ever march home the same way. Take a different route so you won't be ambushed.

AND SO ON—ALL very basic, but rules that are constantly violated every day by military forces. At the cost of blood.

Whatever your job is, you should have an SOP for it. And it should be written so that someone with no background can achieve a base level of functioning in the job for a short period of time. Do a HALO check of the SOP. Does it make sense to someone without insider knowledge? Other SOPs should lay out the way your organization works. The way things really work, not how you want someone to think they work. These are critical when undermanned and when people have to cross train or take over someone else's job.

SOPs are a great way to codify habits you want to develop and also list habits you want to avoid. Writing them down and posting them some place you can consistently see them helps keep you in the real world.

Failure to follow SOPs lays the groundwork for disaster, as is failing to study history.

SOPs should be followed, but also evaluated in the face of changing circumstances. SOPs are not written in stone. SOPs need to be checked every once in a while to make sure that they are applicable and that they are being followed. Having a nice-looking binder with wonderfully written SOPs does you no good if no one reads them or follows them. And SOPs that are out of date can cause more harm than good. They should be constantly updated based on After Action Reviews.

I just read an interesting article that said that hospitals that use 10 item pre-surgery and post-surgery checklists cut their mortality rates in half. Simple things like: Is this the right patient? Is this the right surgery for this patient? Is this the correct arm to amputate? Have we accounted for all our equipment after the surgery?

It's not just the SOPs that are critical. A valuable byproduct is the focus it forces everyone to take.

14

AFTERWORD

The wide range of disasters in this book show that they don't happen in isolation. There are Cascade Events. Any disaster involving humans has at least one, if not more, Cascade events that are human error.

Thus, disasters can be avoided.

The Green Beret Guide

Seven Ways to Prevent Disasters
Have a preparation mindset
Focus
Conduct an Area Study
Use the CARVER formula
Have a 10th Man
Conduct After Action Reviews
Use Sanding Operation Procedures

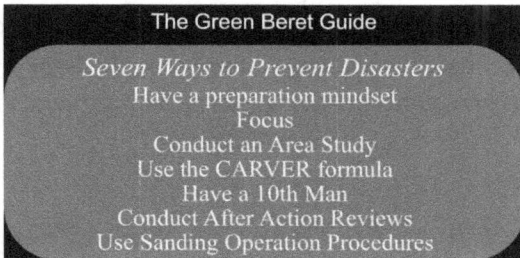

Remember: Shit Doesn't Just Happen!

THE END

THE GREEN BERET PREPARATION and SURVIVAL GUIDE
A COMMON SENSE, STEP-BY-STEP MANUAL FOR EVERYONE
NY Times Bestseller & Former Special Operations
BOB MAYER

The GREEN BERET GUIDE FOR SUCCESS
The Strategies of the Quiet Professionals
NY Times Bestseller & Former Special Operations
BOB MAYER

THE GREEN BERET POCKET-SIZED SURVIVAL GUIDE
First Aid, Water, Food, Shelter, Scavenge. Specific Emergencies and Disasters
NY TIMES BESTSELLER & FORMER SPECIAL OPERATIONS
BOB MAYER

THE GREEN BERET GUIDE to SEVEN GREAT DISASTERS
WHAT CAUSED THEM AND HOW WE PREVENT FUTURE ONES
(VOLUME 1)
Titanic; Little Big Horn; Donner Party; New London School Explosion; The Housing Bubble; Kegworth Plane Crash; Apollo 13;
NY Times Bestseller & Former Special Operations
BOB MAYER

THE GREEN BERET GUIDE to SEVEN GREAT DISASTERS
WHAT CAUSED THEM AND HOW WE PREVENT FUTURE ONES
(VOLUME 2)
Pearl Harbor; Kursk Sinking; Challenger; Sultana Sinking; the Last Tsar; St. Francis Dam Failure; Flight 571 Crash
NY Times Bestseller & Former Special Operations
BOB MAYER

THE GREEN BERET GUIDE to SEVEN GREAT DISASTERS
WHAT CAUSED THEM AND HOW WE PREVENT FUTURE ONES
(VOLUME 3)
Air France 447; Fetterman Massacre; Hillsborough Soccer; A Bridge Too Far; Tenerife Airport Disaster; Deep Horizon; Salem Witch Trials
NY Times Bestseller & Former Special Operations
BOB MAYER

The Pocket-Sized survival guide on the right top, is the same as the Green Beret Preparation and Survival Guide on the left top, minus the preparation portion; sized at 4' by 6' in order to fit in Grab-n-Go bag, glove compartment, kitchen drawer, etcetera.

15

APPENDIX A: THE AREA STUDY
WHAT IS AN AREA STUDY?

(partly excerpted from *The Green Beret Preparation and Survival Guide*)

An Area Study is examining your environment with the perspective of evaluating assets and threats so you can properly prepare. An Area Study will allow you to tighten down your preparation and focus on things in order of priority. It's not just the environment but also includes yourself and your team.

In Special Forces, prior to deploying to an Area of Operations, we conducted an Area Study of that location. You must conduct an Area Study of your Area of Operations (AO). This means studying your home, your work, school, and any other locales where you and people on your A-Team spend a significant amount of time. When taking a trip, you should conduct a travel area study, examining the route you will take, your destination, and your route back.

There are so many cases where a thoughtful Area Study

followed up by the appropriate preparations would have saved lives. Preparation is so much better than reacting. Which is what we're doing now.

Area Studies can have non-emergency uses, such as if you're considering moving to a new place. An Area Study can provide valuable decision-making data.

You want to examine your environment for a lot of things. What can harm you? What can help you? What can hide you? What are your enabling factors? What are your disabling factors? What is the terrain and how can it help you or hamper you in movement? What are the roads, trails, rail, etc. What effect does your environment have on you? What effect will you have on it?

In essence, an Area Study requires you to invest some time and energy on research and to look at your surroundings from a different perspective. It can actually be a fun experience and allow you to see the world around you with a different perspective. Get your team involved because we all look at things a little bit differently.

WE LIVE and work in a variety of natural and man-made environments. There are a wide range of human developments from urban to remote rural. Thus, one size doesn't fit all.

Doing an Area Study is critical so you can tailor your preparation for your specific situation. Some threats are going to be of much more importance for you to prepare for than others. For instance, if you live in Oklahoma, the threat of hurricane is nonexistent (so far), but tornados and earthquakes are likely.

The first step is to start with the most important factor: you and those in your A-Team.

The Mild Area Study

Purpose. Delineate the area being studied—this applies to your home, your work, and any other locations you will likely be. We'll start with you, your home and then expand outward.

YOURSELF AND YOUR TEAM

What special skills and background do you have? The people on your team?

These include medical, construction, problem solving, military, the list is basically about coping with a mild emergency that isn't life-threatening. The key is to know what you can and can't do, and what those around you can and can't do. Think back to the last emergency experienced—what was the reaction? The answer to this will give a heads up to how one will react in the next emergency. There is no right or wrong answer, but awareness helps.

These skills include medical, military, gardening, hunting, survival training and experience, pilot, boat operation, camping, weapons, cooking, land navigation, swimming, communication (personal and technical) construction, problem solving, fire starting, knot tying, the list goes on and on. Think back to the last crisis encountered. What was the instinctual reaction? Some people can react well others panic. This is a reality that has to be factored into any scenario.

Task Four: Mild: Evaluate & list the following for you and each member of your A-Team.

Name:

ABILITY TO REACT IN AN EMERGENCY:

SPECIAL SKILLS BACKGROUND #1:

SPECIAL SKILLS BACKGROUND #2:

SPECIAL SKILLS BACKGROUND #3:

SPECIAL SKILLS BACKGROUND #4:

~

OVERALL PHYSICAL CONDITION

This includes ability to walk, how much of a pack one could carry, physical disabilities, allergies, medical status, special needs, etc.

Task Five: Mild: Evaluate and list the following for you and each member of your A-Team.

Name:

   Overall Physical Condition:
   Medical Status:
   Allergies:
   Medications:
   Ability to walk/run:
   Swimming ability:
   Able to drive? What types vehicles?
   Work-relates skills?
   Cross-trained skills:
   Special Needs:

By looking at these checklists you can see what assets and liabilities you and your A-Team have.

Your Home/Work Environment

When we think survival we picture someone out in the

wilderness in a pine tree lean-to, but we spend most of our time in our home and it's easy to overlook what we can do to make that environment safer. It is far more likely, in fact a given, that you will experience one of the accidents or emergencies listed in this section.

When I research I find statistics that are all over the place because people can't agree on definitions. Once more, those statistics are variables that differ from home to home, so I won't quote many (those of you with pocket protectors and calculators can google them) but let's do an Area Study for your home in terms of the most likely areas of concern.

1. Falls are a leading cause of injury and death. This is more likely based on the previous part of the Area Study: your personal physical condition. Older people, naturally, are more susceptible to falls and getting injured. One in three people 65 or older will suffer a fall leading to serious injury, if not death.
2. Poisoning goes in the opposite direction for susceptibility: it is more likely for children to be seriously hurt or killed by ingesting a toxic agent.
3. Children are also susceptible to choking, suffocation, drowning and scalding. This includes airway obstruction.
4. Water leads to drowning. Do you have a pool? Water nearby?
5. Fires and burns are very likely.

Your Immediate Area of Operations
That's a fancy way of saying the area around your home, your work, your school, etc. At HomeFacts you will get a listing of the following which will help: crime rate, environ-

mental hazards, crime stats, drug labs, air quality, radon, UV index, brown fields, registered polluters, tanks and spills, average monthly temperatures, probability of earthquakes, hail, hurricanes and tornadoes; closest airports, FCC towers, fire stations, hospitals and police stations.

Task Twelve: Go to Homefacts
http://www.homefacts.com/ and enter your zip code.

∼

Task Thirteen
Mild: Of the four type of special environments, which ones do you need to be concerned with in order of priority:

Cold Weather, Desert, Tropical and Water

~

HERE IS a partial list of natural disasters:

Tornado, Hurricane, Heat Wave, Drought, Wildfire, Blizzard, Earthquake, Tsunami, Volcano, Mud/Landslide, Flooding, Tidal Surge.

BELOW IS a partial list of man-made disasters.

CAR ACCIDENT, boat/ferry accident, train/subway accident, tall building evacuation, fire, power outage, burglary, robbery, carjacking, civil unrests/riots, terrorist attack, active shooter, firearms accidents, nuclear power plant accident, nuclear weapons, dam failure, biological weapons and infectious diseases, chemical weapons/accident, industrial accident.

WHILE SOME OF them are truly accidents and can't be anticipated, others might have a higher likelihood depending on where you live such as a dam failure or industrial accident. Some also depend on your lifestyle such as where you work or whether you own firearms.

Are your power lines buried? What industries are in

your area? What are you downwind, downstream of? What toxic materials and/or gases would be emitted if there was an accident? Where is the closest nuclear power plant or storage area? Are there labs in your area that work with dangerous biological agents? What about the local university? Are you in the flood zone of a dam breaking? There are many more dams in the United States than people realize. The St. Francis dam disaster is covered in the next book.

Check: http://nid.usace.army.mil/cm_apex/f?p=838:12

FOR THIS WEB site just enter an organization type (any will do) from the drop down menu and you'll be taken to the next page where you can check dams by state. There is also an interactive map.

What rails lines are near you? What is being transported on those lines? Is toxic material being carried? If a train derails and that material is released, what should you do? Under survival, the proper response for a chemical agent is covered—your first instinct to run is usually the wrong one! The same is true for evaluating potential problems on waterways and roads.

Where is your hundred year flood line? You can use the FEMA flood map search to determine this by entering your address: https://msc.fema.gov/portal/search

ALSO, note that recent surveys indicate flood data is changing rapidly.

Here is the link to an article indicating where things are changing:

. . .

HTTPS://WWW.BLOOMBERG.COM/GRAPHICS/2020-FLOOD-RISK-ZONE-US-MAP/

THIS IS BECOMING MORE and more important!

Task Fourteen: Mild: Natural and Man-made disasters in order of likelihood in your AO

Natural Disasters in your area in order of likelihood?

   1:

   2:

   3:

   Man-made disasters in order of likelihood in your AO

   1:

   2:

   3:

   4:

   5:

16

APPENDIX B: DEFINITIONS

The Green Beret Guide

Cascade Event

An event prior to the disaster which
contributes to it,
but by itself is not disastrous.

The Green Beret Guide

The Rule of Seven

Most disasters require seven things to go
wrong.
If humans are involved, at least one
of those seven cascade events
involves human error.

The Green Beret Guide

What is a Disaster?

The final event of the dramatic action,
especially of a tragedy.
An event causing great and often
sudden damage or suffering.
Utter failure.

The Green Beret Guide

The Gift of Failure

What we can learn from past disasters
in order to prepare for and
avoid disasters in the future.

The Green Beret Guide

Delusional Mindset

When someone continually has success beyond
the norm, is helped by an abnormal amount
of luck, and believes the abnormal is normal
and that this 'winning streak' will continue
indefinitely.

The Green Beret Guide

Lose-Lose Training

Aka: *Kobayashi Maru* scenario.
A training scenario where there is no
'right' or 'good' solution.
The goal is to understand how someone
thinks and decides.

The Green Beret Guide

Murphy's Law

What can go wrong. Will.

The Green Beret Guide

Disaster Mindset

Expecting that what can go wrong. Will.

The Green Beret Guide

The HALO Effect

Looking at something from 'outside the box' which gives a fresh and unique perspective that isn't prejudiced by prior experience and knowledge.

The Green Beret Guide

House Rules

The problem with playing by your own rules is that reality eventually catches up to you. No person is larger than the world around them. Reality trumps House Rules.

The Green Beret Guide

Cascade Stopper

A person designated as the check and balance
on a leader or organization, especially
under stressful situation.

The Green Beret Guide

Advice Filter: Does the person giving it:
Have a bias?
What is their goal? Does it align with yours?
Do they have the proper experience to give it?
Do they have a pecuniary stake in you following
the advice?
What is their goal?

The Green Beret Guide

Sunk Cost

A past cost that has already been incurred and
can never be recovered.
It should not be a factor in current
decision-making.

The Green Beret Guide

The Three Stages of Change

1. Moment of Enlightenment
2. Make a Decision
3. Maintain Sustained Action

The Green Beret Guide

Self-Correcting Mindset

We shrug off a physical symptom or an anomaly in our environment and assume it will fix itself.

The Green Beret Guide

WINDHANDEL

Is a "wind trade" because nothing tangible is being traded.
Other than the money.

The Green Beret Guide

Calculated Risk

When one factors in the possibility of everything going wrong and has a disaster plan in place in case it does.

The Green Beret Guide

Positive Response

When instituting critical changes in a system, instead of assuming the changes have been made, a positive response is required for every change.

The Green Beret Guide

System Fracture

A small problem that is the harbinger that
something is wrong. And will get worse.
System fractures do not get better on
their own. Only worse.

The Green Beret Guide

Sixth Sense

The subconscious mind picking up real signals
from our five senses that we are not
consciously aware of, and putting them
together to warn us.

The Green Beret Guide

CARVER Formula
Criticality
Accessibility
Recognizability
Vulnerability
Effect
Recuperability

The Green Beret Guide

Seven Ways to Prevent Disasters
Have a preparation mindset
Focus
Conduct an Area Study
Use the CARVER formula
Have a 10th Man
Conduct After Action Reviews
Use Sanding Operation Procedures

17

APPENDIX C: CHANGE

(partly excerpted from The Green Guide for Success: The Strategies of the Quiet Professionals)

How can you change?

- You have a moment of enlightenment
- You make a decision to take a different course of action from what you've been doing
- Commitment to your decision leads to sustained action, which brings about permanent change

E XERCISE: Which of the three parts of change do you think you have the greatest difficulty with?

. . .

MOST PEOPLE TEND to say *Sustained Action*. However, if you really examine yourself, you might find that isn't your real problem. For example, I have a hard time making a decision. Once I make a decision, I'm very good at sustained action. *Here is the key:* you must not only figure out what step of change you have the most difficulty with, you also have to determine why that step is your problem. The reason I have problems making decisions is because I'm *afraid* of making a mistake. Do you see how the underlying fear is the thing you must uncover?

MOMENT OF ENLIGHTENMENT.

A moment of enlightenment comes in several ways:

1. You experience something you never experienced before and it affects you.
2. You experience something you've experienced before, but you experience it differently and it affects you.
3. You experience someone else doing something differently and it affects you.

NINETY-NINE PERCENT of what people do day-in and day-out is habit. Habits are extremely difficult to change. Think how many conscious decisions you make in a day and how much of what you do is the same thing you do every day. To have a moment of enlightenment you have to become open-minded, one of the character traits we talked about earlier. You must try to change your point of view or perspective. Get out of your rut.

. . .

WAYS TO HAVE **moments of enlightenment**

Can you look at someone who is different from you, who has different values, and not only understand him, but empathize with him to a certain extent? I think many smart people have a hard time understanding others who do things that are obviously not smart. Yet those same smart people have blind spots in their personality where they do corresponding not-smart things. Two things to keep in mind: one is that a moment of enlightenment might come from seeing something and making what appears to be a bad decision; second, when something others do bothers us, it is often pointing out a truth about us. A truth we don't want to see.

As a writer, one thing I constantly do is research. An elite person is always looking at the world around them, trying to see previously unseen possibilities. The more information you gather, the more possible courses of action you have. The Area Study is a good way to look at your environment with open eyes.

Listen and observe. Many times, those who are around us are trying to give us a moment of enlightenment but we are ignoring the message. At work, a co-worker might be pointing something out to you which goes by you without notice.

It can also happen at the national level.

An example of an entire country that failed to have a moment of enlightenment despite two decades between wars to do so is France between the First and Second World Wars, while Germany did the opposite. This happened on two levels.

World War I was a static war with massive armies mired

in trenches. However, there were new developments that many failed to pay attention to: the tank and the airplane. France gave little notice to them (they built a lot of tanks but failed to see armor as a decisive, cohesive force), still believing a large defensive frontier was the answer to their problems. They built the Maginot Line, covering the border where they anticipated the Germans to attack. There were two problems with the line. It ignored the impact of the tank and aircraft, and the French failed to fortify their border with Belgium, where the main German assault would eventually come.

The Germans were forced to have a moment of enlightenment given the severe post-war restrictions put on them by the allies. They *had* to be innovative. They also did a lot of research, particularly lifting the ideas of British military strategists such as Basil Liddell-Hart. The British, themselves, tended to ignore Liddell-Hart's theories on mobile warfare that emphasized massing tanks. Hans Guderain not only read Liddell-Hart's books, but put them into practice in training—which took place in Russia, of all places, as the treaties did not allow the Germans to do this in their own territory.

One reason Guderain was listened to by higher ranking German general officers was simple: they had lost the First World War. The defeat had been a disaster. Thus, the generals were more receptive to change. The elements of blitzkrieg, which Guderain developed, directly disobeyed all the principles of war at the time. That's what made it so successful.

The results became very apparent in 1939 when German armor swept through Belgium, around the Maginot Line, and overwhelmed France in weeks.

Get out of your comfort zone. A moment of enlightenment is guaranteed to be an uncomfortable one.

Take a chance and look at something in the opposite way you've always looked at it. Reverse thinking is a very strong tool to help find moments of enlightenment.

Denial often blocks MOEs.

Angers stops MOEs when it is actually an indicator of an MOE.

Bargaining dilutes MOEs.

MAKE a decision

The moment of enlightenment is internal. But it's not change. So is the next step. If you don't make a decision following your moment of enlightenment, the moment will be gone and worthless.

There are two systems for decision-making: intuitive and reasoning. Intuitive deals with emotion. It is fast, automatic, but has a slow-learning curve. Reasoning is emotionally neutral. It is slow, controlled, and rule-governed, but this approach can be rigid.

Is the majority of your decision making based on intuitive or reasoning? Knowing this about yourself is key in understanding how and why you make decisions and why sometimes you make the wrong decision.

EXERCISE: A bat and ball together cost $1.10. The bat costs a dollar more than the ball. How much does the ball cost?

If you used intuitive decision making then you would say the ball costs .10. But it really costs .05.

. . .

EXERCISE: Flip a coin six times. Which is more likely?
Heads-heads-heads-tails-tails-tails
Or
Tails-tails-heads-heads-tails-heads?

NEITHER OF THE above is more likely to happen. However, if you picked the second, you are using the misconception of chance.

Sports players, like chess players, have to trust intuition for speed of decision-making. Writers have to trust their gut, but then go back and use their rationality to edit the work.

To prevent disasters we must use both types correctly. During planning and prevention, we focus on reasoning. Intuitive comes into play when we are in the disaster and can be made into the correct action through prior training (think of the ambush example).

However, despite having a moment of enlightenment and making a decision, we still haven't changed anything.

SETTLE on a sustained course of action to implement the decision.
Don't expect immediate, burning bush change. While this does happen, it is very, very rare. Change is a slow process. It requires dedication and commitment.

Sustained action equals change. Sustained action is training, so therefore we'll discuss the sustained course of action more under Training.

THE PROCESS OF CHANGE.

There are five stages a person or organization goes through emotionally when trying to change. They are:

Denial. There is no problem or need to change.

Anger. How dare someone, including me, say I'm not doing it right.

Bargaining. Maybe if I can change some small things it will make a big difference.

Depression. Yes, I do really need to change the big things.

Acceptance. Which leads to the actual change.

These are the same five stages Kubler-Ross defined as the stages a dying person goes through. This is because you have to in essence kill some part of your old self, your old habits, in order to change. You have to surrender the bad part of you to get to the good part.

This also flows from intellectual to emotional change. We go through all five stages intellectually, and then comes the hard part: keeping up sustained action while going through the five stages emotionally.

THE GREEN BERET GUIDE TO SEVEN GREAT DISASTERS (II):
WHAT CAUSED THEM AND HOW WE CAN PREVENT FUTURE ONES

Pearl Harbor; Kursk Sinking; Challenger;
Sultana Sinking; the Last Tsar;
St. Francis Dam Failure; Flight 571 Crash

Available HERE: www.bobmayer.com/nonfiction

Pearl Harbor

"Should hostilities once break out between Japan and the United States, it would not be enough that we take Guam and the Philippines, nor even Hawaii and San Francisco. To make victory certain, we would have to march into Washington and dictate the terms of peace in the White House. I wonder if our politicians (who speak so lightly of a Japanese-American war) have confidence as to the final outcome and are prepared to make the necessary sacrifices." Admiral Yamamoto, Commander Japanese Navy. (Note that this quote was used extensively for propaganda purposed by the United States by leaving out the last sentence)

Kursk Sinking

"It's dark here to write, but I'll try by touch. It seems like there are no chances, 10%-20%. Let's hope that at least someone will read this. Hello to everyone. There is no need to despair." Captain Lieutenant Dmitri Kolesnikov, commander 7th Compartment (turbine room) Russian submarine Kursk.

The Challenger: OrganizationAL Failure

"My God, Thiokol. When do you want me to launch? Next April?" Senior NASA official on a conference call to the manufacturer of the solid boosters, when they recommended on the morning of the launch that it be postponed.

SULTANA sinking

"If we arrive safe at Cairo it would be the greatest trip ever made on the western waters, as there were more people on board than were ever carried on one boat on the Mississippi River!" William J, Gambrel, first clerk & part owner of the steamship Sultana.

The Last Tsar

"I am not prepared to be a tsar. I never wanted to become one. I know nothing of the business of ruling." Nicholas II, last Czar of Russia.

St. Francis Dam failure

During the Los Angeles Coroner's Inquest, William Mulholland said, "this inquest is a very painful for me to have to attend but it is the occasion of that is painful. The only ones I envy about this whole thing are the ones who are dead." In later testimony, after responding to a question, he added, "Whether it is good or bad, don't blame anyone else, you just fasten it on me. If there was an error in human judgment, I was the human, I won't try to fasten it on anyone else." William Mulholland, chief engineer, Water Department Los Angeles

Flight 571 crash

"It was repugnant. Through the eyes of our civilized society it was a disgusting decision. My dignity was on the floor having to grab a piece of my dead friend and eat it in order to survive.

'But then I thought of my mother and wanted to do my best to get back to see her. I swallowed a piece and it was a huge step - after which nothing happened." Dr. Robert Canessa

Amazon

AMAZON

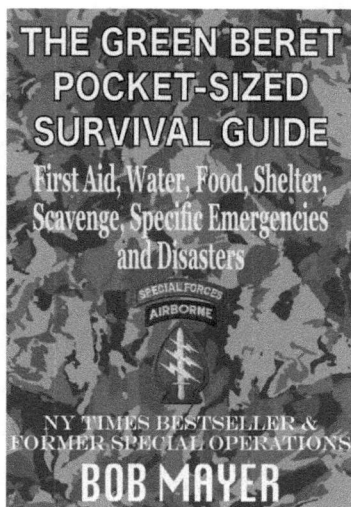

AMAZON

The same as above, minus the preparation portion; sized at 4' by 6' in order to fit in Grab-n-Go bag, glove compartment, kitchen drawer, etcetera.

ABOUT THE AUTHOR

Thanks for the read!
If you enjoyed the book, please leave a review as they are
very important.

Bob is a NY Times Bestselling author, graduate of West
Point and former Green Beret. He's had over 75 books
published including the #1 series The Green Berets, The
Cellar, Area 51, Shadow Warriors, Atlantis, and the Time
Patrol. Born in the Bronx, having traveled the world (usually
not tourist spots), he now lives peacefully with his wife and
dogs.

For information on all his books, please get a free copy of the *Reader's Guide*. You can download it in mobi (Amazon) ePub (iBooks, Nook, Kobo) or PDF, from his home page at www.bobmayer.com

There are over 220 free, downloadable Powerpoint presentations via Slideshare on a wide range of topics from history, to survival, to writing, to book trailers. This page and slideshows are constantly updated at: http://bobmayer.com/workshops/

Questions, comments, suggestions: Bob@BobMayer.com
Blog: http://bobmayer.com/blog/
Twitter: https://twitter.com/Bob_Mayer
Facebook: https://www.facebook.com/authorbobmayer
Instagram: https://www.instagram.com/sifiauthor/
Youtube: https://www.youtube.com/user/IWhoDaresWins
Subscribe to his newsletter for the latest news, free eBooks, audio, etc.

All fiction is here: **Bob Mayer's Fiction**
All nonfiction is here: **Bob Mayer's Nonfiction**

Thank you!